The Children of the South

THE CHILDREN
OF THE SOUTH

Margaret Anderson

With a Foreword by Ralph McGill

Farrar, Straus and Giroux

NEW YORK

This book is for

the Negro children of the South

In every child who is born, under no matter what circumstances, and of no matter what parents, the potentiality of the human race is born again: and in him, too, once more, and of each of us, our terrific responsibility toward human life . . .

JAMES AGEE, Let Us Now Praise Famous Men

Acknowledgments

IN writing this book I have been helped immensely by the editorial counsel and steadfast encouragement of Henry Robbins of Farrar, Straus and Giroux. Without his patience and help, this book would never have been possible. And in the early stages I was helped also by Sylvia Dudley, who was taken ill shortly after the book was started. Her enthusiasm for the project remained with us as an inspiration throughout the writing of the book. I also wish to express my appreciation to *The New York Times* and especially to the editors of *The New York Times Magazine*, in which portions of this book originally appeared in different form.

MARGARET ANDERSON

Foreword

BY RALPH McGILL

WHEN I had read the manuscript of Margaret Anderson's book *The Children of the South,* the fragment of a Proverb intruded into my mind. I looked it up. It was Proverbs 4:23: "Keep thy heart with all diligence; for out of it are the issues of life."

Margaret Anderson kept her heart with all diligence. This chiefly is why this excellently written book will be remembered and kept when many other books coming out of the fever and ferment of the South will be forgotten. It is a book that will be picked up for rereading of well-remembered pages and for the dignity and bravery of children in moments and hours of terror when adults had lost their reason and were mad with the poison of hates. She does well to say, on the dedicatory page, that the book is for "the Negro children of the South." They earned it—at Clinton, at Little Rock, at New Orleans, and other cities and towns of the South.

Margaret Anderson was teaching in Clinton High in 1956. (She still is there. Lucky Clinton.) The U. S. Supreme Court decision had been handed down in May 1954. Clinton's school was ordered desegregated. All was quiet.

ix

There were some who did not like it. And then came a man named John Kasper. He had the gift of demagoguery. He soon became a racist Pied Piper, followed by all those who before had lacked someone to articulate their prejudices, fears, and hates.

Margaret Anderson introduces him and goes on with her narrative, telling of the lives of the people of Clinton—the children, their parents, the townspeople. It is perhaps fitting to say here that there came a day when a federal judge, one of the Taylors of Happy Valley, a family who long before had produced governors and a United States Senator, sat patiently on the bench while Kasper's defense brought out all the ugliness of prejudice that was admissible. It was so bad and there was so much of it that the jury and the townspeople were sickened. Kasper went to jail. Tennessee's Governor Frank Clement sent state troops in to keep Clinton's school open. (He was a year ahead in setting this precedent. A year later, at Little Rock, Governor Faubus sent Arkansas troops to prevent the schools from opening.) Clinton's school later was literally destroyed with an estimated hundred sticks of dynamite. It cost over half a million dollars to replace it. Children in many cities each bought a brick. Voluntary donations helped. The county board of education found extra money.

This is some of the background. But this book is about children and their parents, especially their mothers and grandmothers. It is the story, too, of children who came to school in those early, grim days between rows of cursing, hot-eyed men and vicious, shrewish women whose language was filthy beyond that of men. It tells of the Negro children in the classes and corridors in that first year when children from the homes of the hate-filled men and shrilling shrews brought the same tactics to school. It probes skillfully and deeply into the powerful and melancholy influence of many years of segregation in the South and its impact on the white and Negro population both.

The book goes deeper than that—much deeper. It is good that a teacher should reveal so vividly, weaving her story out of the lives of children, what the costs of generations of segregation were, and are, to some 20 million Americans. Mrs. Anderson places the necessary emphasis on the installments paid on a debt that will take many years to be cancelled out.

Out of her years of experience Margaret Anderson writes:

"The Negro child *is* different from other children, even other children of deprived backgrounds, because he has problems that are the product of a social order not of his making, or his forebears'. . . . The Negro child comes to us [teachers] an overburdened child, taxed in a hundred ways that make him old beyond his years. The road for him is three times as hard as for the average white child, even the poorest white child. Although the poor white child has much in common with the Negro child in that both have experienced deprivation, the Negro has handicaps which do not shackle a poor white child so noticeably. At every turn there is an obstacle, and forever and ever, the Negro child must ask himself, 'Why?' "

I can testify to the accuracy of Margaret Anderson's words. The Negro child, caught from birth in segregation, shut off from the nation's political, cultural, and values system, grew up, almost inevitably, with a low estimate of his own possibilities. It was hard not to have a poor self-image when the child's mind could not conceive of being

xi

much more than what his parents were. Segregation deadened initiative, suppressed personal confidence. Many of these children—too many—came from homes where neither parent could read or write. These and other factors in the long years of segregation created a handicap that even today is not quite fully understood.

Margaret Anderson's conclusions are supported by my own years of work and experience. The Supreme Court was never more right than when it found that a segregated system was and is, per se, discriminatory. It was, terribly so. The agrarian South, with a per capita income considerably below the national level, attempted to carry two school systems, though money was lacking for even one good one. The Negro schools were far inferior. The Negro teachers were, as a rule, less trained, because of the segregated teaching schools. The South has been sacrificing generations of its children. But segregation was more than that. It was, especially in the rural regions, almost total alienation from the community. In some towns and communities the Negro occupied almost exactly the place of the untouchables in India. We are just learning that while segregation was a "system" designed to separate the Negro from the rest of the community, the effect was like that of the "system" of slavery. All who lived in it were affected by it. The Negro, being a minority, was the more penalized. But the white majority could not escape. The results are visible in educational and economic lags as well as in the area of moral convictions and in religious health. The costs will be paid for a long time. The umbilical cord that stretches from the generations of segregation to the slum riots in large Eastern and Western cities is unmistakable.

Margaret Anderson illustrates her findings of the over-all

damage done by segregation with the stories of children in her class. They tear at the heart. Let us take, for example, the story of Roberta. Margaret Anderson met her first when Roberta was twelve. A school census was being taken.

Roberta came to the door. She had a tiny baby in her arms. She invited the teacher in. Roberta's mother had left word about her coming. The house was a low-ceiling hut with three rooms: living room, bedroom, kitchen. There were no closets or bathroom. The floors were of unfinished planks. One could see through the cracks. The walls were papered with newspapers. In the center of the main room was a pot-bellied stove. There was one bed in the house, an old iron bed with a thin, sagging mattress, lacking a sheet. Pallets on the floor served the children.

There were eleven children. The mother had left a notation of the names and ages of each. There had been different fathers, and none was now living with the family. Roberta was in charge. She talked of her keen desire for books and reading. She "couldn't wait" to get to high school. . . . Roberta did go to high school . . . to the school that was once all white. She, "a child hungry for books," wore a dress made of feed sacks and a dingy white blouse. Her glasses, provided by public assistance for eyes too long neglected, kept slipping down on her nose. But for Roberta the material things did not then matter. She was happy, enthusiastic. . . . She scored high on her mental tests. She had determination and will. She would rush home when school was out, always with books, to do a full day's work before sunset . . . and when this was done she turned to her books. In the Negro elementary school she had led. In high school, for which she was ill-

xiii

prepared, she had trouble making average grades. By the second year, the toil with eleven children to care for and the house and the hard schoolwork "to keep up" had begun to do something inside her. But she never asked for help. She went to summer school, working to help pay her way. A new baby was on the way at home. And then Roberta dropped out of school.

Margaret Anderson went to her and asked why.

"I woke up one morning and looked about me," said Roberta, "and I just decided it was too much to overcome."

Margaret Anderson properly asks what is going to happen to all the bright, good minds such as Roberta's. What symbols will these young people look to? To what in their environment will they respond?

". . . The Negro students in today's schools are in the process of becoming what they will be tomorrow. . . . So often have I thought how carefully we would teach them if we were wise. . . ."

This is a book that everyone interested in the tremendous processes of desegregation and integration, and the problems of life and education should read. Margaret Anderson devotes several chapters, based on case histories, to what Southern education needs. Parents of white children who still oppose desegregation of schools would profit enormously from this book. So would congressmen, senators, and all those confronted with educational problems. Much of the white South, victimized and psychologically distorted by generations of segregation, might obtain understanding by reading *The Children of the South*.

It is a book written with much compassion and understanding—out of life and out of the heart of a great teacher.

Contents

The Children of the South

Years of Turmoil

IT has now been ten years since that autumn day in 1956 which proved so different from all the other days on which I ever started a school year.

Some people look upon autumn as the time when the year is moving down the long slope, and they connect it with sadness. But for a teacher, autumn is the beginning of everything. It is a time of hope. It is a time when life takes on new meaning and new purpose, when you have the privilege of starting over and redeeming yourself of the errors of the past year.

A teacher sees magic in the seething turmoil of shrieking school children, skidding bicycles, the pushing and shoving, the freshly ironed dresses, the new shoes. The beginning of school, for a teacher, is like your first look at your new-born child. You take him in your arms, a little afraid, yet resolutely. You know that nowhere else in the world is there a human being exactly like this one, and there never will be. You know that you belong to him and he belongs to you, and you are an integral part of each other. And yet you are separate individuals. You will care for him and teach him, only so that he will be able to leave you and take care of himself. And as you look at him, you know that whatever is strong in him must be nourished and protected. And you have faith that whatever is weak in him can be strengthened.

But this day everything was different. You could almost feel the difference in the air. Today was the day many had said would never come, the day some had sworn they would die before they would see. And it was here. This was the day the children from Foley Hill were "coming down."

The children from Foley Hill, the Negro section of Clinton, Tennessee, had been coming down for a number of years, but in a different way, of course. Some of their forebears were among the first settlers of the town. They had helped to cut down the forests and clear the river banks and build the houses. Now their descendants were coming down, not as laborers or spectators, but as students entering the white children's high school to receive a proper education. The May 17, 1954, decision of the Supreme Court, which had declared that segregation of children in the public schools of the United States is unconstitutional, had finally reached us. And Clinton High School was the first state-supported school in Tennessee to be ordered desegregated, one of the few such schools in the South at that time. Now the groundwork was laid for a "new era" in the education of the Negro children of the South.

It was long overdue.

Since 1619, when a Dutch man-of-war landed twenty Negroes at Jamestown Harbor for sale as slaves, the Negro in America has been struggling to gain that most precious human right—the right to learn. From the beginning, an

4

ignorant slave was considered a safe slave; and to make certain that he remained ignorant, the Southern colonies and later many of the states passed laws denying the Negroes the right to an education.

In the years before the Civil War, many slaveowners were willing to allow their slaves to learn to read the Bible, but they lived in fear that the slaves would also come to read Abolitionist papers and literature. They knew that with education the slaves would become rebellious and hard to handle. A Virginia legislator in the early 1800's is said to have informed his colleagues: "We have as far as possible closed every avenue by which light may enter their minds. If we could but extinguish the capacity to see the light, our work would be completed. They would be on the level with the beasts of the fields."

But the slave-owning South never succeeded in extinguishing the desire and capacity of the Negro for learning, any more than the Greeks were able to keep the slave Aesop from telling his stories; or Terence, a Negro, from writing plays. Despite slavery, many Negroes did manage to acquire some learning. They listened while their mistresses read stories to the children of the household. Some borrowed or stole blue-back spellers from the big house and learned to read by memorizing simple words. Some, in isolated areas, were taught by Christian missionaries.

The most privileged of the Negro children were those who came to be called the "playboys." The selection of the playboy was a big event on the plantation. The children were called up from the slave cabins to perform for their mistress. They ran, jumped, turned somersaults, recited, and sang to impress her with their talents. From among them, one would be selected as the special playmate for the young master. The "playboy" would be cleaned, scrubbed, and put into a "tow linen" suit. He would stay in the big house much of the time; and, if he was a satisfactory playmate, eventually he would become a trusted house servant. This was a coveted honor.

But the number who had such advantages was small. Any attempt to provide systematic education for the Negro was opposed vigorously by the majority of the whites, whether slaveowners or not.

"Learning will spoil the best niggers in the world," the Southern white man contended when he found a slave learning to read. Frederick Douglass, a Maryland slave, demonstrated that there was truth in these words. His mistress had taught him to read, little knowing the desire she was kindling in him. Douglass later led an antislavery movement, became a noted lecturer, and founded an Abolitionist paper, the *North Star*.

After the Civil War, a system of universal free education was set up in the South, which hitherto had had few public schools. It had been traditional for the children of wealthy families to attend private schools; the poor whites and the Negroes remained illiterate. It was not until after the First World War that publicly supported schools for Negroes began to receive any serious attention. These schools were operated under the "separate but equal" doctrine going back to a Massachusetts case of 1849 in which the courts sustained the validity of the "separate but equal" schools in Boston.

By the 1930's it became clear that in most states the emphasis was on "separate" rather than "equal." The inequalities were glaring and Negro organizations began to seek help through the courts. Many Southern states moved frantically to put more money into building, improving, and equipping Negro schools, even at the expense of the white schools, in an effort to keep the schools segregated. But the economy of the South could not, it seemed, bear the burden of two separate school systems.

Then on May 17, 1954, came the epochal, unanimous decision of the Supreme Court that voided the "separate but equal" doctrine and declared that segregation in the public schools of the United States was unconstitutional.

Clinton is a mill town of approximately five thousand people located on the banks of the Clinch River, in the mountains of east Tennessee. It is seven miles from Norris Dam, one of the great TVA projects; and seven miles from the atomic research center of Oak Ridge. My husband and I had come to make our home here from the mountains of eastern Kentucky, where we had both taught school after the war. I had returned to teaching in 1953 when Clinton High School needed a teacher for a business-education course who could also take over a class in American history.

The spirit and morale of the staff and the students were so fine that I thought it was the most wonderful school I had ever known. Students and teachers were free to explore new ways of teaching and learning; the school was noted for its student leadership; the faculty was outstanding. One teacher had just returned from England, where she had been a Fulbright scholar; and many others had traveled extensively. I felt it a privilege to be associated with these people.

The original law suit petitioning the courts to allow Negro students into the school had been initiated in 1950 by local Negro citizens with the backing of the NAACP.

There was no Negro high school in the county, since the Negro population was not considered large enough to warrant it. The few Negroes who did attend high school (from ten to fifteen children a year) were transported to a Negro high school in Knoxville, twenty-five miles away, at the expense of their parents and with some help from the county.

"I just can't pay out all that money," a Negro parent said. "If they can't go here, they can't go." As a result, many Negro students, even though they were within the compulsory school age, never attended high school at all.

From 1950 to 1956, the County Board of Education exhausted every legal means to prevent desegregation. When the federal court ordered the school opened to Negroes by the fall of 1956, there was an atmosphere of general concession.

Although almost all the teachers had been brought up and educated in the South and had not taught Negro students before, it did not occur to anyone to do other than obey the court order. They did not all approve. But no one wanted to place his personal feelings above the ruling of the court. After the final judgment, there were few people in the community who spoke openly against the Negroes coming into the school. Horace V. Wells, editor and publisher of the local newspaper, kept the people informed concerning the coming desegregation of the school. He published stories, under bold headlines, announcing the event. There was no public reaction.

That there should ever have been racial conflict in Clinton is something of an enigma. The people of the town could not be called "typical" Southerners. There are few remnants of Southern aristocracy or wealth—the ante-

8

bellum homes, deep drawls, magnolias, and such that one usually associates with Southern tradition. Agriculture had consisted, for the most part, of hillside farming and had not called for a great deal of slave labor as in the Deep South. During the Civil War the people of the area had remained loyal to the Union. The state of Tennessee seceded, but Northern sentiments were so strong in east Tennessee that the region threatened to secede from the state and rejoin the Union.

On August 20, 1956, a Monday, both the Negro and the white students registered for classes. As was the custom, the school was then dismissed for the remainder of the week while teachers attended meetings and made plans for the year. Classes would start officially the following week. Insofar as is known, no white children were kept at home because of the Negroes. The school enrollment was higher than the year before. The Negro children seemed to be accepted by the white children. White students greeted those Negroes they had always known, in friendly and informal ways, as they had all their lives. A Negro girl was chosen to be an officer in her class. A Negro boy expressed his desire to participate in intramural basketball practice. No one objected. D. J. Brittain, the principal of the school, told us: "If we can get through the first two weeks, we will be all right." I wondered why he expressed apprehension when everything was so peaceful.

Then, on the weekend before school was to reconvene, a long-faced, slovenly dressed man arrived in town, seemingly from out of nowhere. He slept in his car that first night. And then he began a door-to-door campaign circulating vicious literature. He approached housewives at work in their yards, men in their garages, and asked in a soft compelling voice: "Do you want your child going to school with niggers?"

Some told him to move on. Others listened. He urged them to picket the school and conduct a mass meeting; he asked students to boycott classes. Before nightfall, he had obtained the signatures of dozens of people in support of his plans. Word circulated quickly that a man named "Kasper" was going to organize a mob to keep the Negro children out of the school.

Now there seemed to be no turning back. The movement John Kasper started spread rapidly. Many people were persuaded by him. The first public meeting he called was attended by twenty-five or thirty people. Within hours after that, there were many strangers in town; and cars from Alabama, Georgia, Mississippi. Whoever Kasper was (and nobody really seemed to know), he had recruited men from all over the South, including a radical segregationist from Birmingham, Alabama, named Asa Carter. These people created enough disturbance so that on August 25, a Sunday, the local authorities arrested Kasper on a charge of conspiring to incite a riot. On Monday morning many people, including some of our students, picketed the school with signs: "We don't want to go to school with niggers."

That morning the twelve Negro children started their lonely trek of no more than half a mile down the hill to the white school. By the end of the week they had walked into newspaper headlines all over the world. Newsmen and photographers descended upon the small town. Men and women with hate-contorted faces lined the narrow streets and shouted at the children: "Niggers—coons—go back to

Africa! You'll never stay in that school!" And each morning the twelve children marched straight ahead in a body, seemingly unmindful of those who shouted vile names. The boys led the way and the girls followed close behind them.

The people who lined the streets to jeer at the Negro children came early, even before the school personnel arrived. They parked their cars and got out and waited. Among them were women carrying babies in their arms. They would mill about on the streets waiting for the Negro children to start down the hill, and when the children came in sight, someone would shout, "Here they come!" Inside the school, the white students waited at the windows, watching the Negro boys and girls in their ordeal.

"Bobby was our hero," the Negro students said later of the oldest among them. "He was the one who went first—the one the white folks picked on—the one who waited for us in the afternoon until the last one of us was safely out of the building."

But Bobby Cain, a quiet senior, was not always as brave as he appeared to his classmates. He told reporters he didn't really want to go to the white school, because he didn't want the white people to hate him. He knew the town was said to be basically opposed to desegregation and actually unprepared for it. But his mother told him that she'd had to "push" for what little education she had and that, if he didn't stay, his brothers and sisters wouldn't have any place to go. The family could not afford to transport all the children to a school away from home.

At night, Bobby would go home and sit and tremble and brood. Then, he said, he'd take an aspirin to calm his fears, go to bed and "pray to the Lord to help me get through that line the next morning."

That week, John Kasper was quickly freed in the Trial Justice Court by a local jury. His followers, who packed the courtroom and carried signs outside, cheered. Immediately after his release, Kasper came to our school, not more than a block away from the courthouse. A crowd of about a hundred and fifty people had been milling about all morning. The principal went out on the lawn to try to reason with him and keep the mob out of the school building.

Inside, the children listened and watched. They discussed what they would do if the mob came into the school to get the Negro children, who sat and waited in their seats with almost frozen expressions. White boys edged toward the doorways and managed "conveniently" to find seats in front of and to the side of and behind the Negro boys and girls. It was a spontaneous, undirected gesture of brotherhood.

In spite of the principal's efforts, the crowd outside became unruly and it seemed advisable to take the Negro children home for their own protection. During the week, school attendance dropped by about half. People were afraid to send their children to school. The parents of the Negro students left work to come for their children also.

"We love our children, too," a Negro mother said. "I just can't understand it. We've always gotten along before."

One day, during those violent weeks, there was a soft knock on my classroom door. It was Olivia, the grandmother of one of our Negro students. She was trembling. Beads of perspiration rolled from her forehead.

"I've come to get Jodie and take him home," she said. "I'm afraid for him to go alone now. All day at work I've listened on the radio to the things they're saying. I couldn't do my work. Finally, I just said I would have to leave and get my boy."

Olivia continued almost breathless. "I don't understand it," she said, pointing to her hands. "You know yourself as well as I do, if I rub this skin off right here, we're the same inside."

"I know, Olivia," I said. "I know—" But I didn't know whether I did or not.

"Maybe it's best Jodie does go with you," I said, for I was mindful of the mounting trouble in the streets. I asked her to come inside the room, but she said she preferred to wait in the corridor. Then I went to tell Jodie that his grandmother was waiting for him. Without questioning, he began to gather his new books, his pencil and paper. The other children looked on.

"May I take this?" he asked, pointing to some work he had finished in class.

"Certainly, Jodie," I said.

Then, very pleasantly, he asked, "What are we going to do tomorrow?"

"Tomorrow, Jodie?" I couldn't answer. I know that no child's question should go unanswered. I had to answer, but the words wouldn't come.

Looking back, I think it was perhaps at this moment that I came face to face with the twentieth century. I had been brought up in a Southern community in Kentucky where there is much more of the "old South" atmosphere than Clinton had ever known. We had a large Negro population and it was quite segregated.

The Negroes lived in a part of town known as "the Kingdome." I do not know how "the Kingdome" got its

13

name, but there the Negroes were "lord and master." They had their own churches, their own undertaker, a beauty parlor, a grocery store, and a dilapidated school. Most of the Negroes lived in cabins owned by whites. These were seldom improved. Some had screens on their windows and doors, but most did not. Some of the Negroes owned their own homes, which usually had small picket fences around the front yards. And it was a rare home that in the summer was not graced with flowers of every color bordering its porch. And not many were without a huge woodpile in the back yard, near which there was always a big black iron kettle filled with "white folks' " washing.

There was no talk of "segregation" or "integration." These words were unknown to us. We accepted whatever frailties or virtues the Negroes had, and they seemed to look on us in the same way. We lived apart, but in basic acceptance of each other. For all I knew, this was the way the Negroes wanted it.

My father was a country lawyer, and in my youth I had heard him plead to juries in defending a Negro: "You must not let the color of this man influence your decision . . ." But these words had no real meaning to me then, nor did I understand why it was necessary to make such statements.

Even amid what I suppose was blissful apathy, there is one thing I am most grateful for, because it provided a basis for the future. The white people in the community I grew up in were always kind to the Negroes, and the Negroes to the white people. At least, this was what I felt. There was never anything like what I had seen these past few days.

Then I heard Jodie repeat: "Tomorrow—what are we going to do?" And something took hold. I thought of the vicious people outside, with no purpose other than to destroy, and of the children inside, who had come to learn. No, one could not make right out of this. It was too out of tune. The words then came. "Why, tomorrow, Jodie, we're going to work just as we did today. Only every day will be bigger and better from now on. You'll be here?"

"I'll be here," he said. "I've come to stay with you."

He walked slowly to the door. Olivia stepped forward to meet him and lifted her big checked apron to throw around him. "Come on, Jodie," she said, "my old apron's dirty and the spit won't hurt it."

By the end of the first week of school, the crisis had mounted. A restraining order had been served on John Kasper to curb his activities; but now Asa Carter, even more effective as an agitator, addressed a crowd of approximately fifteen hundred people. There was a sudden silence when he stepped to the front of the courthouse steps wearing a black suit and no tie.

"I'm Asa Carter," he began. The crowd cheered.

"I'm from Alabama." The cheers grew louder.

"I came here because I want to help you start a white citizens campaign in your town. . . . We're Anglo-Saxon. We make up thirty percent of the population. For every three white men there are seven colored men on this earth. But you'll find that the Anglo-Saxon races are the only ones that have ever maintained a free government for free men."

Then he attacked the Supreme Court, and law and order. There were shouts from the audience, "He's right," and "Tell 'em, Asa." He talked about a white-citizens council, and while he talked, some hundred and fifty people paid $3 each and signed up. Then Asa Carter from Alabama slipped away into the night.

By 11:30, the mob had taken over the town. Cars passing through the streets bearing Negro passengers were overturned. Photographers and newsmen were attacked. "The only picture we want is a picture of a nigger with a noose around his neck," split the sultry air. Our police force, then six strong, was almost powerless. They had had no experience in handling mobs.

On Saturday, civic-minded townspeople decided to form an auxiliary police force. They called it the home guard. They armed themselves with shotguns, rifles, pistols, tear gas, and night sticks. They were determined to prevent another night like the night before.

But people continued to gather in the town that Saturday afternoon. The forty-seven men who constituted the home guard tried to keep the crowds moving on through town. At one point, when a mob of about two thousand refused to move, the forty-seven dispersed them with teargas bombs. But the crowd formed again. The townspeople were terrified. Many stayed inside their houses. "What's going to happen to us," they said, "when neighbor starts fighting neighbor?"

Public officials pleaded with the governor for help. Finally it came. Shortly after dark, a hundred state troopers, members of the highway patrol, in thirty-nine cars with red dome lights flashing and sirens shrieking, poured onto the bridge over the Clinch River leading into town. The patrolmen maintained order through the night. At noon on Sunday, they were relieved by six hundred national guardsmen in tanks and armored cars. This was called "Operation Law and Order." They were more than welcomed by the law-abiding, peaceful citizens.

For the time being, there was quiet. The Negro children

1 6

entered and left school under the protection of national guardsmen. On September 4, a United States Deputy Marshal stood on the school steps and read a federal court order placing the entire citizenry under a federal injunction. This took place just outside my classroom. It seemed like a nightmare. Only two weeks before, there had not been even an undercurrent of trouble. And the worst was still to come.

The court order kept the crowds away from the school building. But elsewhere the Ku Klux Klan paraded boldly and held mass meetings. They congregated on farms outside the town, formed motorcades and drove in a procession, blowing their horns wildly. One night they held a huge meeting and burned three crosses on a vacant lot off the main highway. There were speakers from all over the South. It was like an old-fashioned revival meeting, and anyone who felt compelled to talk was invited to the speaker's stand. Their voices were amplified so they could be heard across the river and in the town.

During October and November there was a lull in the violence, although the meetings continued. It was difficult to maintain order in the school because of the tension in the community. The segregationists were now acting in other, even more effective ways—pitting child against child, neighbor against neighbor, and even members of a family against each other. By December, school conditions had also deteriorated. The Negro boys and girls had suffered such persecution and humiliation at the hands of the few white antagonists who seemed uncontrollable that they decided not to return to school until they could be guaranteed protection from bodily harm.

"We don't want our children to get hurt," said the

mother of one of the boys. And another added, "We had a meeting and we decided we are not going to send our children back until the school board promises it is safe for them to return."

It was on the morning of December 4, as the Negro children stayed in their cabins on Foley Hill, that the Reverend Paul Turner, the tall young preacher at the First Baptist Church, reared in Southern traditions, made a historic journey. This was the morning of the city election. The segregationists now had sufficient strength to present a candidate for mayor of the town. That brisk morning, while angry crowds waited about, word came that the preacher had gone up the hill to bring the Negro children back to school. He was accompanied by two of our leading citizens. Crowds milled about the school in defiance of the injunction. Inside and outside the school building, everyone waited to see what could happen.

"He'll be killed!" a woman cried.

At 8:15, the little group came in sight. The Reverend Paul Turner walked solemnly down the middle of the street with the children on either side of him. "Don't be afraid—don't be afraid," he said softly to them. "And were you afraid?" I later asked one of the children. "No, ma'am," she replied. "We were not afraid with him." As they neared the school, they looked neither at the unshaven hecklers nor at the women lining the streets. The hecklers seemed thrown off guard by the daring of the act and did not move toward them. The little group reached the steps, the preacher turned and with the children walked straight into the school. He delivered the children to their classrooms and then walked out of the building, his dark coat over his arms, and started back to his church. He was not smiling. He walked straight down the front steps and past the angry people cursing him, aware that they were following. Before he reached his church, he was cornered and attacked, his nose was bloodied and his face cut. But as one eyewitness remarked, "That preacher put up a good fight."

Word spread rapidly that the preacher had been attacked. People were indignant. This act of violence seemed to bring the situation into focus as nothing else had. From all over town, people rushed to the polls—many who perhaps would not have gone otherwise.

School activities were disrupted. People from the streets would come in to create disturbances; it was impossible to hold classes. The principal's wife, a home-economics teacher, was accosted when she attempted to keep out two boys who came "looking for niggers." At lunchtime the school was closed again. "We are going to close the school today, close it tomorrow, and close it until it is safe for children to attend," the principal said.

Some students cried. "Does this mean we won't graduate?" they asked. "Does this mean we can't get into college?" They bitterly resented the outside interference that had upset their lives, and expressed their bitterness more than they ever had before. "We could have handled it if they had left us alone," they said. "Why won't they leave us alone?"

"I thought I didn't want the Negroes. Now I don't know. I wouldn't want to be like those people out there," said one of the white boys.

"I feel sorry for the Negroes," said one of the girls. "We just ought to show those out-of-towners who've come to make trouble."

The teachers were hesitant to leave. They stayed and

19

drafted a public statement, their first. Neither the faculty nor the majority of the students wanted the school closed. They knew the closing of the school would be interpreted as a sign of defeat. And they were not willing to accept defeat.

That night, when the election votes were counted, the White Citizens Council, it was found, had been defeated by an overwhelming majority. Some said it was because of the preacher. "Isn't right to beat up a preacher," they said. Then came the counter-comment: "Isn't right for a preacher to interfere in things outside his church."

In his home that evening the minister told reporters the purpose of his mission: "I accompanied the Negro students to school to try to let my presence be testimony that as long as the law is what it is and as long as they [the Negroes] have a desire to go to the school, it is their moral right to come unheckled and unhindered." On Sunday morning Paul Turner was back in his pulpit, his face swollen, and he spoke to a large crowd. "There is no color line at the cross," he said.

The remainder of the school year was comparatively quiet. Somehow, some way we managed to finish the year and provide a minimum of education for the boys and girls who wanted to learn and who could learn in spite of everything.

Six of the twelve Negro children stayed with us all year. One, listed as a "gifted child" by the elementary school she had attended, moved away with her family. She was the girl who had been chosen as class officer at the beginning of the year. Her father said, "I don't believe there will be an opportunity for my children in Tennessee because no matter how much education they get there's no place to use it." One Negro boy was graduated—Bobby Cain.

Before the graduation ceremonies, word came that some of the hate-mongers were going to try to keep "that nigger" from going through the line. Bobby with his quiet dignity and courage had won the respect of many of the white children in his class. The extra police force that was called out that night, to be on hand in case of trouble, was not needed. "He's going to get his diploma," the white boys said. "He's earned it." They planned among themselves how they would defend him if anyone tried to take him out of the line of graduates. But nothing happened.

Bobby became the first Negro to be graduated from a state-supported white high school in Tennessee. The other Negro children said, "If Bobby can do it, I can, too."

In the spring the principal announced that he was leaving. He described his feelings in a television broadcast:

I can frankly say that I've suffered nothing but personal harassment, and other people have too. My wife and teachers and students in school, and anybody that took a stand to obey the law . . . I guess my life was threatened ten or twelve times by anonymous telephone callers who would hang up . . . My wife and I, since the opening of school, are always careful when we go home. We study the premises. When we get in, we lock the doors and get the lights on . . . It just presses you down every day lower and lower. To me, it is an amazing thing that an American citizen living in the United States has to be subjected to this, while the lawless citizens, those who refuse to abide by or accept the law, continue to run free . . .

And Tennessee lost one of its finest educators, a man who had devoted his life to the boys and girls of the county, as his mother and father before him had devoted their lives to the teaching profession. The faculty was torn apart. Before another year passed, only seven or eight of the original staff of thirty members would be left. Many moved away. My husband and I thought perhaps we should leave also. We had our children to bring up. The most we could ever hope to give them with a school-teacher's salary was an education. Certainly, this was no place now for that. We were offered better positions elsewhere. Friends and family advised: "Get out of it." But something made us feel we should stay.

The next fall, five of the Negro students from the previous year returned, and there were three others. The walls of the school had withstood that first year, but the spirit and the heart within were shattered. Deep resentments had carried over from the year before. It would take a generation, it was said, to overcome the animosities generated in the first year of desegregation. The Negro students were coldly received. And there were many incidents.

A new administrator from an adjoining county was selected for the school. He accepted the challenge of a position that most people would shun, and he has since proved his courage. W. D. Human said, on arriving in the town, "I don't anticipate any trouble in my school." Anyone who saw this dark-eyed man, with slightly graying hair, tackle the situation the first day could not doubt that he meant to have order. He dedicated himself to one purpose: maintaining a school for all the boys and girls. It was not an easy task. It was difficult to get replacements for the faculty members who had left. He had to accept applicants with no experience, some even without state certification to teach. In some classes there was a turnover of from three to five teachers during the year.

But that year we began to feel that once again we might look forward to working on the serious business of educating our children. Law-abiding citizens were in charge in the community. There seemed to be less concern that a few Negroes were attending the school and more concern about the quality of the education the town's children were getting in an atmosphere of tension and turmoil. It was still hard going for the Negro students. Three of the eight who enrolled transferred to a Negro high school in another county, and one withdrew. One girl was graduated. One of the boys who went back to attend the tenth grade in the all-Negro school began to lose his eyesight that year because of a brain injury at birth or in childhood, and before his death at twenty-three became totally blind. "Tomorrow isn't promised to me," he had told his family.

We immersed ourselves in our work and tried to forget the past and start over. Plans were set underway to improve the old building, and money was appropriated to modernize the science department, which had had no new equipment in twenty-five years. Carpenters wiped off the vicious language on the walls and desks and covered the holes in the walls—remnants of a school gone wild a year before. We were beginning to feel respectable again.

The following year, the third year of desegregation, we started school calmly and in an orderly manner. Thirteen Negro children enrolled. Some were brothers and sisters of the children who had come the two previous years. It was easier for them. There were no lines of people to greet them, no crosses burned at night. We were grateful our children were in school and that we had a school. But the stillness was portentous.

Sunday morning, October 5, 1958, the town was blanketed in a heavy fog from the river. Without warning, the school was ripped apart by three massive explosions which rumbled through the town. So adeptly, so "professionally," were the seventy-five or a hundred sticks of dynamite placed inside the building that the structure was almost completely destroyed. People stood in the streets in the early hours of the morning and looked on the wreckage in anger and grief. "Oh, my God," an old man said, standing on the courthouse lawn and looking across at the debris. "I never dreamed it would come to this."

"What if there had been children in there?" a mother asked. If the explosion had occurred at that hour one week before, there would have been: a hundred and twenty boys and girls of the high-school band, of which my husband is the director. They had just returned from the Southeastern Music Festival at Bristol, Virginia.

The Negroes, in their cabins just above the school, felt the tremor of the earth and ran out of their homes in fright. "I tell you, it was awful," said one of the women. "It was just like two worlds coming together."

The blasts tore away partitions, lifted ceilings, plummeted steel beams through the desks, blew out doors and windows, crumpled walls. There was glass everywhere. Hundreds of books were ruined and would not be replaced for the rest of the school year. The new principal said, "I've been a school man all my life. This is like a death in the family."

That Sunday morning the school was roped off. Large

signs were placed on the lawn: Danger—No Trespassing. The water mains were stopped, the utilities disconnected. Policemen stood guard to keep hundreds of curious people away from falling brick. For parents and teachers, who have so much of themselves in the youth of the community, more than a building was roped off. This occurrence was no less vile than Hitler's order to burn the books in Germany, or the Russians shooting down college students in the streets of Budapest. "How could this happen in America?" we asked.

By nine o'clock that morning, before the dust from the explosions had settled, public-spirited citizens and school officials began to plan for a new school. They did not know just how or where, but their children were going to have a school. And the plans did not exclude the Negroes. The town was united and strong in its purpose.

On Monday morning at 7:45 the faculty met in a dark and cold gymnasium. They left no doubt that they would carry on. The students arrived at the regular hour, and the Superintendent of Schools, James A. Newman, who had only a few weeks before taken office, spoke to them for the first time. "I have been knocked down," he said, "but never knocked out." The students applauded enthusiastically.

For three days we held "school" in the open air while officials made preparations to accept the generous offer of the people of Oak Ridge that we use an abandoned elementary school owned by the government. It was thirteen miles from our school. Trucks were donated and maintenance crews supplied. Furniture from undamaged rooms was moved to the new quarters, and the government provided additional furniture, to replace what had been lost. Students helped move the salvaged furniture; mothers dusted the desks and scrubbed the floors, washed windows and woodwork. Two hundred volunteer workers accomplished in three days what would normally have taken weeks.

On Thursday morning eight hundred children were transported to the new school, which we were to use for two years. In the buses, they sat three deep or stood in the aisles. The students were met by Oak Ridge officials and by the ninety-piece Oak Ridge High School Band, which had stood for more than an hour in the dew-covered grass. Representatives of the Boy Scouts of America raised the American flag over the school, which is high on a wooded hill. The president of the student body, a youngster from a farm family, accepted the keys to the building and unlocked the door. He was so moved that he could barely speak.

"Perhaps," the students said in the first school paper they put out in the new school, "time will erase the initial feeling of loss, the feeling of physical sickness that one or several persons would have so much hate and venom that it would destroy reason. Out of evil does come good, strong school spirit, a feeling of oneness; a welding together of school, community, and church; a co-operative, concerted effort to re-create . . ."

The community was as one in their desire to rebuild the school, and quickly. Deeply moved, the columnist Drew Pearson visited the ruins and met with leading citizens to see about starting a fund-raising campaign to help rebuild the school. He proposed as a slogan for a Clinton Schoolhouse Fund: "Buy a brick of friendship to combat bombs of hate." "The thing that stands out in my mind," Drew Pearson said, "is the crass disregard for the most important natural resource we have in the United States—our children." Pearson organized a nation-wide committee consisting of distinguished Southern leaders. Within a week, his efforts on behalf of the children of the town began to show results, and eventually a large part of the cost of the new building was defrayed through the generosity of people all over the world, of thousands of school children who went without a Coke or a movie to "buy a brick of friendship," and the determination of a community of good, fairminded citizens who would not permit an act of terrorism to impair their children's education.

While we were consuming our energies in petty hatreds, the Russians launched their Sputniks. Congress, recognizing the inadequacy of our preparation for a new age in which survival would depend upon scientific knowledge, passed the National Defense Education Act. This act, an emergency measure, provided among other things for guidance programs in the public schools, and for guidance counselors—people who would devote themselves to helping youngsters plan their education, decide on careers, jobs, college, and help too with their personal problems. In short, they would help every child make the most of himself and his opportunities. No school in our county had ever had such a program.

When the state supervisor suggested that I should start this program in our school, it was like a dream come true. I could see the great need for trained counselors in any school at any time, and most especially in a newly desegregated school, to help guide both the white and the Negro children in the period of transition. Though I had two college degrees, I still did not have the education required;

2 7

so I went back to the university to receive the necessary training. That year I tried to carry two jobs at once and attend school at night. I knew that the new guidance program had to be good so people would understand the tremendous need for it and never again feel that their children could do without these special services. When we resumed classes in the new school then, a special office had been set aside for "Guidance."

Ever since, I have worked as a counselor with both white and Negro children, but the Negro children seemed to present such special problems that I became very close to many of them. I helped them adjust to the new school, plan their courses, discover their talents and develop them, find ways of going on to college or trade and technical schools, secure jobs, and cope with their many personal problems. Some days we just talked and planned for a better world. For a decade now, I have witnessed their struggle and been a part of it. In a sense, I became their captive. And I could not free myself of them and their problems, for my conscience would not permit it. Their struggle became my struggle, their successes were my successes, their failures my failures.

Frequently people would ask: "Why are you so concerned about the Negro children?" At times I was almost made to feel that there was something wrong in caring. But then I would wonder: How can a teacher watch children struggle and not be concerned? Is one's Christian conscience only for Sunday morning? Here is an opportunity to exercise not only Christianity but our love for our country and everything it stands for. Have these no meaning when put to the test? How can a teacher see any "color" in a child—anything but the heart and mind in the wondrous, glorious "process of becoming"? Are not these, too, American children who come under our flag and for whom we are also responsible?

It has seemed that within the past decade we have, of necessity I suppose, been so preoccupied with the physical process of "getting the Negro children into the white schools," or else "keeping them out," that we have overlooked the impact of this social upheaval on the children themselves. When, in fact, it was for the children of the nation that the Supreme Court found it necessary to reach down and extend a helping hand. By its ruling of 1954 it showed that it was as concerned about the liberties and opportunities of the smallest, blackest child as it was about those of his parents.

During the past years a number of questions have occupied my thinking, questions that I would like to consider in the chapters that follow: What happens to the Negro children in these circumstances? What happens to the white children? How are they affected? And, most of all, how can we help them in this great social transition?

2

Tote the Weary Load

A^s Negro children enter our schools in increasing numbers, we are able to see at first hand the effects of
slavery and deprivation upon a people. Reading about it in
history books is one thing; looking into the eyes of children, hearing children talk, and feeling their tears, is quite
another. And some days during my years at Clinton, when
I've tried to cope with the problems of Negro children, it
has seemed to me very much like watching three hundred
years of humanity reaching up and saying: "I want my
chance. I want my chance." The chant reminds me of a
deep, dark, silent river going back centuries—older than
any of us.

It was on a warm spring morning that I went to Roberta's house to take the school census. I knew of Roberta
from my visits to the Green McAdoo Elementary School,
where I had often talked to the Negro children. Her
teachers had pointed her out as an unusually intelligent
child with an inquisitive mind. I had never been in her
home.

There was no school that day and several children were
playing hide-and-seek in the yard. When I asked for Ethel,

Roberta's mother, two of the youngest boys rushed into the house, I assumed to tell her that "the teacher had come." Instead, Roberta came to the door. She was then about twelve, and she held a tiny baby in her arms. She asked me to come in.

The house was a low-ceiling hut with three rooms: living room, bedroom, and kitchen. There was a small hallway, but no closets or bathroom. The floors were of wide, unfinished planks, now worn slick, and one could see through the cracks. The walls were papered with newspapers.

In the center of the main room stood a huge pot-bellied stove with an elbow pipe extending out of the wall just below the ceiling. Although it was a fairly warm day, the stove was so hot it was difficult to breathe. On top of the stove there was a pan filled with steaming water. Occasionally the hot ashes from the bottom of the stove sifted out through the openings and onto the bare floor.

There was one bed, as we think of beds, in the house. It was an old iron bed with a thin, sagging mattress and no sheets or covers on it. The other "beds" were pallets placed in the corners of the room and piled with dirty, patched quilts and blankets. Around the pallets were pieces of board about six inches high that gave a boxed-in effect. They looked like the kind of frame one might make for a child's sandbox. The dining table was made of wooden crates and had a checked oilcloth thrown over it. The main room contained a dingy couch, a huge chair, and a television set.

Before long, the little ones began to emerge from almost everywhere, to be in on this "important business." Everybody who could find room sat on the couch in a row. The others stood. Roberta held the baby in one arm and with the other hand reached over to the mantel behind the stove for a paper.

"Mother knew you were coming," she said, "and she left this for you before she went to work." The paper gave the names and dates of birth of the children. There were eleven, including the baby, now a month old. I tried to copy the names as best I could. I soon learned that the children had different fathers, and not one of the fathers lived with them now. The family situation was so confused that I didn't have the heart to ask any questions.

Ethel would not be home until late in the afternoon. Then there would be food in the house. She would take her day's earnings and go to the grocery store and the children who had been "good" would be allowed to go with her. Roberta was in charge and she would make the report. One of the little boys was very quiet and did not seem to be feeling well. Roberta said he had been hot all morning. I felt his head; he seemed to have a fever. "I have no way to call Mother at work," Roberta said, "but if he isn't better by the time she comes home, we'll get some medicine."

The children were glad to have company, so I forgot the census and we had a visit. All in all, they seemed quite happy. The boys were jovial and had funny things to say. Roberta was more serious.

"They're going to learn," she said, pointing to the boys sitting on the couch. "I learned to read before I started school. They had to move me up a grade, I was so far ahead of the others. Then I read everything in the elementary school library, and ran out of books." The boys looked at her in a sort of awe and then looked at me and laughed. Roberta went on to explain about her liking for books, and what books she had read. She said she couldn't wait until she got to high school to read new ones.

But how would she ever fully realize her talents, encumbered as she was? Could books make up for her home environment? It just didn't seem right that life should be such a struggle for a child. I was glad she and the others were too young to know. Soon, of course, they would.

"I'll be waiting for you next year, Roberta," I told her when I left.

Holding on tight to the baby, she waved goodbye and replied, "I'll be there."

I could not get her out of my mind. In America—in the twentieth century—across our back fences—there was a child "waiting for books." I had seen her and talked to her, and I would get her an armload of books now, whatever she wanted. If other people knew, they would do the same. But even that would not be enough.

Roberta was perhaps unusual, both because of her talents and because of the extreme difficulties she was faced with. Suppose we take a look at a more nearly "typical" Negro child. And here you may wonder, as I have often wondered, whether, except for the color of their skin, there is really very much difference between a Negro youngster and a white youngster. And why, once the Negro child has the right to come into the white schools, he cannot be transformed instantly so that he can be on a par with the white children.

We know all Negro children laugh uproariously. They push and shove, and play ball on the common. They wish on the stars. They feel sorry for children in other parts of the world—as I know the children in Uganda and Poland feel sorry for the Negro children in my town, because they wrote to them to say so. Negro children delight, too, in tinseled angels on Christmas trees. And they cry when they're hurt. They have the problems that come with physical growth, the problems of getting along with their parents and with other boys and girls, or succeeding in school and fitting into an adult world, of learning to understand themselves. Then how are they different?

The Negro child *is* different from other children, even other children of deprived backgrounds, because he has problems which are the product of a social order not of his making, or his forebears'. This social order is so impressed upon him that it is reflected in his way of life, his outlook, his mannerisms, speech, and dress. Because of slavery, which still haunts us, the almost indelible imprints of sub-servience and deprivation are upon today's Negro children. And because of this deprivation, the Negro child comes to us an overburdened child, taxed in a hundred ways that make him old beyond his years. The road for him is three times as hard as for the average white child, even the poorest white child. Although the poor white child has much in common with the Negro child in that both have experienced deprivation, the Negro has handicaps which do not shackle a poor white child so noticeably. At every turn there is an obstacle. And forever and ever, the Negro child must ask himself, "Why?"

One of the most noticeable of these handicaps is the Negro child's low estimate of himself and his possibilities. In his mind, he conceives of himself as never being much more than he is now, or than his parents are. He starts out assuming that he will fail. He knows white people will be astonished if he succeeds. This is not simply a neurotic attitude. There are very real reasons why the Negro child has a low estimate of himself and his opportunities. He is the product of a home background and of a society that fostered the suppression of initiative on his part. His parents have been victims of suppression, and many have adjusted to an inferior status; the child knows little else but to feel the same way. It becomes a normal way of life for him. Of the more than one hundred Negro children with whom I have worked closely, no more than five expressed real confidence in themselves and their abilities when they came into the white school.

This child's parents probably cannot read or write well, if at all. Few have ever been to the polls and voted—not always because they could not (as in some states), but because they know it is not expected of them and they feel no civic responsibility. And not many Negroes own their own homes: they have not had sufficient income to purchase property. They may live in a two- or three-room rented house, often dilapidated. There are usually many children in the family—ten or twelve perhaps. Frequently, the mother is the sole support of the family. She works as a domestic and is paid little, and may not even be regularly employed.

The parents do not spend much time with their children, as middle-class white parents do. There may be no one to read to the children, or sit and talk with them. There is no money for books and newspapers. In the rural South, Negro children are, more often than not, retarded in school one or more grades. Except for their church, they have never been included in community activities. They stand on the sidelines and yearn to participate.

The Negro child writes words as they sound in the dialect he speaks. He makes all kinds of errors, and people laugh at him and imitate his ways. His teachers have difficulty understanding him and consider him slow. In time he learns to say very little in class. "I'm afraid to speak out," a Negro girl said. "They don't expect me to know anything, so usually I just say that I don't know." This attitude is common among Negro students. They feel inferior to the white children with whom they find themselves in competition. And too often they hide their feelings or accomplishments under a mask, doing what they think other people expect of them.

When a person is given a certain role in life, or a certain social position, especially during his formative years, he comes to accept this as his true place. He comes to believe that he is just what the people around him think he is. Only the very strong in mind and spirit are able to overcome this environmental handicap without help. The brilliant Negro students, who are capable of accomplishment, tell me how they struggle against this feeling of being less than they are.

Thomas, a tenth-grade boy, provided an example of the low estimate the Negro child seems to have of himself. When I sent for him to come to my office—I wanted to talk with him and get to know him—he was scared something was wrong, even though he couldn't think of anything he had done wrong. He seemed afraid to sit down. When, at my suggestion, he finally did, he stared down at the floor and fumbled nervously with the pencil in his hands. No one had ever sat down with him before just to talk about himself, about Thomas, which to a fourteen-year-old boy is the most important thing in the world.

"Do you realize, Thomas," I said, "that what you have accomplished here indicates that you are a capable student and that you have a very real artistic talent?" I talked to him of ways in which he might explore this talent. He raised his head and looked at me for the first time. "Nobody ever told me I had anything good about me," he said. And that was all he said. I thought he had not realized the importance of what I had tried to tell him, as there was no other response. But a few days later he came back. "Let's talk about that drawing business," he said.

Randolph was another Negro boy who downgraded himself. All through high school, Randolph never once indicated that he had any desire to go to college. Whenever I talked with him about his future, he said he wanted to "join the service." After graduation, and just before school started in the fall, he called one day to ask to have his papers sent to a college. He said he had worked all summer and had made enough money to be able to start college. If we had only known he wanted to go to college, we might have been able to help him—by obtaining financial assistance and, even more important, by preparing him more adequately for higher studies. But on second thought: whoever behaved as if Randolph could or would go to college? He had merely played out a role. We expected nothing of him; we saw nothing of him—that is, until after graduation. All the while, this boy had secretly yearned to make something of himself. He just didn't know how to let us help him; and he cannot be blamed.

Thomas and Randolph were typical Negro students who had been brought up in an environment that served as a constant reminder that the road ahead would be hard; that, in fact, there was little they could look forward to in life. They knew very few people who had not had a difficult time merely subsisting from day to day. This had produced a deep insecurity; they would never accomplish anything, they were certain of that. I am happy to say that for these two boys there has been a change. Thomas is exploring art to his heart's content, and Randolph is doing well at college. With remedial classes, he came through the first year, and now he is trying to earn enough money to return. But so many are not this fortunate!

It has been said that one of the reasons why the Negro in America has placed so much emphasis on life after death is that he has little or no hope for comfort in this world, so he has turned his hopes of experiencing real happiness and fulfillment to heaven. Only recently, I visited the home of one of my students whose father had died after a long illness. There were many things in Kathleen's home that morning that made my heart heavy. One was the sight of a dirty yellow envelope nailed to the wall inside the front entrance of the house. The envelope had contained the insurance policy, and, as is often the case in Negro homes, it was nailed near the front door so that it would always be available when the collector (one of the most important people in a Negro child's life) came on Saturday morning. If the mother was away, the children would know how to take care of the payment. This morning the policy had been removed from its envelope and taken to the funeral director as proof of the family's ability to pay for his services.

It occurred to me that this piece of paper represented the kind of security Kathleen's family could never hope to have in life. This day the children had seen the powerful force exerted by that paper on the wall. Their father would have a decent burial. And everybody had new shoes for the occasion. They were taking them out of the boxes when I arrived. They almost seemed happy about it all.

The feeling that there is little in life he can look forward to seems to be almost ingrained in the Negro child. It casts a shadow over everything he does. And in addition he carries another burden which is the product of the times and which those who work with him need to understand. The Negro child comes into the desegregated school in what we might call a "state of marginality." That is, he is on the periphery of two very different ways of life and in the process of crossing from one culture to another, very much as the children of immigrants might strive to learn to move freely in a new society. This seems strange indeed when one considers that America has been the home of these people for so long, that this child and even his grandparents have never known any other home, and that there are deep bonds between the two peoples, that we live side by side.

In my community, only a few years ago, the Negro and white children played ball together and together went hunting for chestnuts and persimmons on Saturday mornings. Many a Negro child was reared in a big house on Main Street because his mother had to bring the baby with her when she came to work, and in order to get Negro women to come, the white women would provide a nursery for the little ones. Yet today I hear Negro children saying as they approach a white school, as if they were entering a new world: "I worried about what I would wear when I came down here." "I wondered if I would know how to eat in the lunchroom." "I wondered if I would look to suit them."

Last fall, after nine years of desegregation, I walked over

to a group of Negro children huddled in the corridor amid hundreds of white children on the first day of school. "Do you understand how to get to your first class?" I asked them. They replied that they did but said, "We're afraid."

"There is no need to be afraid now," I chided them. "If you had not come, we would have sent for you."

But these were empty words. Their answer to my question and the very fact that they had come as a body and remained huddled in a group indicated the inner conflict these children were experiencing as they struggled to cross over into a new way of living. This struggle is intensified by the fact that these children are actually living in two very different environments at the same time. One is the world of the new school, where everything is new for them. The other is the home, which represents ignorance, deprivation, and the old way of life, to which they return after school.

This "marginal state" can be very disturbing for anyone, although it does not have to be. The Negro child tells us (and the social revolution and his people about him dictate) that he will never, never again return to the old ways. That is, he thinks he will not. If he is forced to, it will not be as the same individual. We might as well accept that. He will never suffer the indignities his forebears suffered. Yet there is a struggle, for he is not quite ready to enter wholly into the "new ways."

Nowhere is the turbulence that arises from the Negro's marginal state more evident than in the young people. One college student put it this way: "We've come a long way. We're better educated than our parents. We can read and write. We know more about what is going on in the world. We get around more. It's hard now even to visit back home and be happy." The young Negroes are dedicated to change. I have seen it even in very young children. Becky, I thought, expressed this determination with simple eloquence. She is a beautiful girl with a gentle face and a soft manner, and she moves with grace and poise. One day her teacher asked her to play the part, in a school play, of a Negro servant of the old days. The teacher had hoped thus to befriend the child; she thought this was an opportunity for Becky to participate in a meaningful activity.

"This part," the teacher said, "was made for you."

Becky looked over the script, which contained dialect such as was spoken in pre-Civil War days: words such as "mawnin' " for "morning," "gwine" for "going," "dis" for "this," and "bees" for "is." The child returned the script to the teacher, saying, "No, ma'am, we don't talk like that no more."

The teacher tried again: this was really the heroine's part. "You see, Becky, the part was made for you," she said. "You are the only one who can do it. Everyone will love you for it."

The other children in the class looked on. They had written the play, and because they wanted Becky to be in it, they had created this part for her. It was the only role that seemed real to them for her.

The thin young girl looked at the teacher and insisted respectfully, "No, ma'am. We don't talk like that no more." And no amount of persuasion could change her mind.

Becky is a child in a "marginal state." She was born into one culture, one social group—the old-fashioned Negro group—and knows little else. Quite suddenly she has been thrust into a new group. But she retains so many of the distinguishing marks of the old culture (the dialect, mannerisms, incorrect English) that she is not yet recognized as belonging to the new. Herein lies her dilemma and her hope: she has made up her mind that she is coming out of the old group, the group with which her parents are associated. She is no longer to be referred to as "May's girl," or "Emma's girl," as it was the custom to call Negro children. She is Becky—an individual in her own right and out to make her own way in a new world. It is as if she had left home to seek her fortune; and never, never again will she return to the age of the rural "folk Negro." This was plain for all to see.

The Negro child's actions while in this "interim" state can lead him to success or failure, happiness or despair. He can come to realize ambitions he did not dream were possible; or he can experience a defeat that leads only to degradation. It is a challenging time for Negro youth, and a treacherous time.

The Negro child must overcome still another obstacle. He comes to us seemingly with little racial pride and social status, and practically no family heritage. He becomes very conscious of this, perhaps for the first time, in the desegregated situation. He now finds himself in a society that talks only of itself and of its accomplishments—a white man's world where people of his color have at best been tolerated rather than accepted seriously or looked to as any significant force. This child cannot associate himself with anyone who holds an important position in the community. Often, the only professional people with whom he has had contact are his minister and the Negro teachers at the segregated school. This lack of racial pride and social status increase his feeling of inferiority. He is also deeply concerned with his lack of immediate family heritage, especially in small Southern communities, where ancestry is important.

Since I came to my own work with Negro children with no professional training in race relations, I have often sought the advice of successful Negro teachers and administrators when I faced a complicated problem. And I have found them most helpful. I first met Frances, a brilliant young teacher, when we attended classes together at the university at Knoxville. I always admired her frank, clear-cut way of explaining things. And I sought her help when I needed it.

"You have a family heritage," she said one day. "We have none. You can tell me who your mother and father were, and your grandmother and your grandfather. We can go back so far and then everything is hush-hush." Frances laughed, but there was irony in her laugh. I knew what she was talking about. Her words brought memories of an incident in my childhood concerning another Negro who stands vividly in my mind. We called him "wise old Will."

Will was said by many to be the richest and wisest Negro in our part of the country. He could neither read nor write. When I first knew of him, he was past seventy. His mother had been a slave. Will was born in slavery and did not know his exact age, as is the case with so many of the old Negroes; but he said he had figured from events he could remember that he must be between seventy-five and eighty years old. Old Will came to town once or twice a year to transact his business at the bank and to buy equipment and supplies for his fertile, river-bottom farm. He brought his money for deposit in paper sacks. When he

43

came to town, the lawyers, doctors, and merchants stopped work to talk with him. It was not uncommon to see him on one corner of the bank, surrounded by prominent white men—talking, asking questions, all enjoying themselves.

Will knew about politics and economic trends. He could quote poetry. He spoke intelligently about Communism, socialism, and the New Deal. He talked about ways to conserve the land and the forests. He was like some prophet of Biblical days. One day after school, I happened by my father's office when Will was visiting. My father and he were old, dear friends, and this office was always Will's last stop in town. It was here he came to rest when his business was completed.

"Will, you are the wisest Negro I've ever talked to," I heard my father say. "You cannot read or write, yet you have amassed a fortune in a poor county . . . Down there on your farm you've figured out the problems of the world . . . white men seek your counsel."

Will just sat there in his cane-bottomed chair and smoothed the little patches of white hair on the sides of his bald head and chuckled proudly.

"Who are you, Will?" I heard my father ask.

There was a pause. Will looked up and across at the volumes of law lining the walls, as if somewhere in those pages there must be an answer. His words echo across the years. "I wish I knew," he said. "I wish I knew."

Since those days, I have taught children who might well be the grandchildren or the great-grandchildren of "wise old Will." And when Negro children have told me of their deep feelings regarding their family heritage, as they often do, it has never been hard to say: "You will make yourself a name. And we will begin right here—this minute, this

44

day. You can build for yourself and your family a noble heritage, so noble that no one will need to ask who you are."

But it is not as simple as all that. I know that the whole structure of the Negro family, the conditions under which these children are born and grow up "like Topsy"—unrecognized and neglected—must be changed. In any child's development, the influences of home and family outweigh all others.

The increased concern over poverty in the United States has in recent months brought to light some startling facts concerning the Negro family, mainly because Negroes constitute a large portion of the population currently described as "disadvantaged." National statistics on birth, death, unemployment, disease, health, broken homes—practically everything generally recognized as contributing to the instability of the family—indicate that life for the average Negro family in America is hard by any standards.

The average Negro mother may not know that she is four times more likely to die in childbirth than the white woman. The Negro child can expect his father to live seven years less than the average white man; and between the ages of thirty and sixty the death rate is twice as high for the Negro as for the white man. The Negro child will also learn that his father's chances of being unemployed are four times higher than the white man's. The health of Negro children is also a major problem. Vast numbers suffer from malnutrition. This is evident in the condition of their teeth, the frequent colds, and the lack of physical strength. I see few Negro children who have ever had a complete physical examination. And only when pain is excessive do they visit a dentist. Often, by the time the child is in high school, his teeth are almost beyond repair.

There are other conditions in the home of this child, who seems to have the cards stacked against him from the day he is born, which can be as detrimental to his development as bad health, lack of medical care, and poor food. Because of inadequate housing, crowded living conditions, and ignorance, the children see a great deal of the seamy side of life. They may live amid drunkenness and debauchery. In their earliest years, the children are brought face to face with the worst aspects of life. Many of them never know anything else. One need only listen to Negro children talking among themselves to realize how much of this they absorb and how naturally they use obscene language, for example.

The average Negro home in the South is a permissive place where the children come and go as they please, and they are expected to be out on their own in their early teens. Parents have little privacy, and the children have no place to go off alone and study or play. Negro youngsters tell me it is nearly impossible to find a place to concentrate and study at home. "How can you study," they ask, "with children crying all around and the television blaring?" I have known Negro students who stayed in school after hours or returned to the library at night because they could not study at home.

Real fun and recreation seem to be lacking in so many Negro homes. The children have no place to go but the streets for their games. "My greatest ambition," Marie once said, "is to grow up and make something of myself and come back, and one of the first things I would like to do is to build a playground for these children so they wouldn't have to move out of the street every time a car comes by."

Mealtimes, which afford a family an opportunity to be together and enjoy each other's company, are not that in the average Negro home. In many homes I have visited, the mother just places the food on the table and the children eat as and when they come in. Sometimes they merely grab food from the table and take it outside. If the mother works, she may cook the night before and leave the food for the children to eat the next day; or she may just let them make out as best they can. Good table manners are, oftener than not, almost nonexistent. It is not uncommon to find Negro youngsters in high school who have never used a knife or fork in eating—only a spoon. I do not mention these shortcomings in a spirit of criticism—but we must face facts.

This kind of family life, which is characteristic of so many Negro families today—though not all—is not without cause. No history, however complete, may ever be able to tell us all the ordeals the Negro family in America has been subject to. It has been, more or less always, in a state of upheaval, of instability. And we see the effects of this instability in the Negro children of today.

In the beginning, when Negroes were captured in Africa and brought to America in chains, there was of course no semblance of family life for them. Members of families who were captured together were separated. The tribal customs under which these people had lived for centuries were obliterated overnight. This itself would be a traumatic experience.

Under slavery, the preservation of the family group was of no great concern to the slaveowners. Some, of course, were kind and allowed families to remain together. But if separation served the economic purposes of the slave-owners, mothers and fathers were separated and sold individually, along with the livestock, in public gatherings at an auction block. Families, such as they were, lived under constant fear that they would not be allowed to stay together.

Few slaveowners were concerned about the physical comforts of their Negroes—that is, not any more than for their best livestock. This would have meant building the slave cabins some distance from the big house, raising them off the ground a few feet to insure proper ventilation, and making certain that not too many slaves slept in one cabin. The farm journals of the 1850's and 1860's are full of articles recommending sanitation and cleanliness in the slave quarters because so much time was lost due to sickness and diseases among the slaves.

Only a few of the Negroes were advanced to positions as "house servants." Most of the Negro men served as "field hands" and were looked upon as the lowest form of life. Many thought of themselves as such. Booker T. Washington told of having talked to an old Negro from Alabama who had been sold in 1845. "How many of you were sold?" Washington asked him. The old man replied, "There were five of us—my brother and myself, and three mules." The field hands were rarely permitted to leave the plantation. It was the only world they knew.

The Negro mother was the most stable member of the family. When the slaves were auctioned, she was more likely to be left with the children than the father was, perhaps because the survival of the children often depended upon her, and children were considered a capital investment. A healthy Negro child between the ages of six and nine would bring from $150 to $300, and his value increased up to the time he was middle-aged. Then, too, Negro women showed such a fierce attachment to their children that when the masters threatened to take them away, the women became a force to be reckoned with. There were many stories of mothers who killed their children and then committed suicide rather than be separated from them.

The Negro woman was important in other ways too. There are instances in which the masters had women bred as they did their stock. And women bore children frequently, thus increasing the master's investment. Few plantations did not boast of a Negro "mammy" in the big house who reared the white children.

After emancipation, the Negro family underwent another great upheaval. The vast majority of Negro men and women roamed the country, looking for homes and work. But women with children found that they had to settle in one place in order to take care of the youngsters. The mother, then, would make a home for them as best she could while the father "followed the North Star," an expression used both before and after emancipation for the Negro's efforts to find his way north. Often he did not return to his family. At this time, a household often consisted of the Negro mother and her children, the grandmother, and the middle-aged daughters, married or unmarried—all living under the same roof, with no men in the house. Under these circumstances the Negro woman was of necessity the head of the family.

The matriarchal family structure has persisted to this day. Emancipation did not bring economic security and opportunity for the male Negro, or an end of discrimination in employment. The Negro woman, however, could always rely upon domestic employment to support the family, and she continued to be looked to not only as the main breadwinner but as the spirit and strength of the family.

She has borne her burden well. Since I have been working with Negro children so closely and have had an opportunity to talk with outstanding Negroes all over the country, I have realized the extent of her influence on her people. Surely, when the history of our times is written, her name will have a special place.

The Negro mothers and grandmothers who worked in the "big houses" of the old South absorbed a great deal of the culture they came in contact with—the fine manners, the kindness and gentility we like to think are characteristic of Southerners. Even in the direst poverty, Negro mothers try to instill some of this in their children. Frances, the schoolteacher whom I mentioned earlier, is a tribute to her mother's influence. One afternoon I called and asked if I might come and talk with her. She was most gracious. That day she delved deeply into the privacy of her own spirit to share with me some of the ordeals her people have endured.

"My people were simple folk," she said. "They were domestic workers, but they had a high sense of values. They were clean and church-going. My parents together made twenty dollars a week and sent us to high school and college. That will give you some idea of the sacrifices they made because of the things they believed in."

"You know," she went on, "I really believe my mother thought she was not as good as the white folks. But in a subtle way, I think she tried to get over to us that our lives should be a little better . . .

"Why, I can't recall when she didn't have a few rare pieces of china. She always served us with the best things. If there was a broken piece, she used it herself. She felt we should know how to use the best."

Before I left, Frances showed me through her comfortable home. She served ice cream and coffee in china which was beautiful enough to grace a mansion. Then she showed me all her china and crystalware which she had collected over the years, and in which she took great pride. It seemed right somehow that Frances now had the beautiful things her mother must have dreamed of.

The point I wish to make, however, is that in talking to any Negro who has accomplished something of importance, in reading the biographies of great Negroes, one will always find mention of the deep influence his mother had in his life—and even more so, his grandmother. In many instances, it was the grandmother who reared the children while the mother worked outside the home. The Negro grandmother is a "power unto herself." She holds an imposing place in the family. And because of the instability of the Negro family even today, one often finds the old grandmother in the process of rearing a "second family"—the children of her children. When the parents go north, or migrate elsewhere to find better jobs, the children may very well choose to stay in the South with the grandmother.

"I think more of my grandmother than I do of my mother," a young Negro student said. "She's the only mother I have ever known. I wouldn't leave her for anything. She is just living to see me through school."

No one will ever know the sacrifices these women have made for their families. In the old days they endured and suffered in their effort to hold the family together and to keep their children alive. Today they struggle in another way—to see that their descendants realize the equality and opportunity the older generations never had or dared hope for.

A matriarchal structure has been necessary for the survival of the Negro family, but we know that it is not the most desirable way of bringing up children. Boys are particularly affected by the lack of a strong father model on whom they can pattern their lives. A young boy should be able to look up to his father with respect and admiration. In the years I have worked with Negro children, I have known only two families in which the father is looked to as the central force in the household. In both instances, the father has a skilled job and provides for his family.

Boys in a matriarchal society nearly always reflect the attitudes and ambitions of the mother. How many times have I heard a Negro boy say, "I will have to talk with my mother about this!" He never mentions consulting with his father. Or he might say, "My mother says I should stay in school . . ." "My mother says I should go on . . ." "I wouldn't be back to school if my mother hadn't wanted me to come." The father seems to have little to do with family decisions.

The girls are affected too. All too often they have to bear the responsibility for the younger children while the mother goes out to earn a living. There is nearly always one girl at home who has to stay out of school to take care of the smaller ones. Soon they have missed so much school time that they drop out altogether. The girls often marry young, and the young men they marry are not prepared or trained to earn a living. This perpetuates the cycle of poverty and deprivation that their mothers endured.

The Negro family has gone through another kind of

upheaval since World War I, an upheaval accentuated in the years since World War II. As the nation has moved from an agricultural to an industrial society, the Negro has migrated from the farms to the urban areas of the South, the great cities of the North, and in recent years to the West. The mother and the children frequently are left behind and must provide for themselves. When the father is able to take the family to the city with him, they are forced to live in already overcrowded slums. Many Negro families newly come to the cities, like many poor whites from the South, are never really happy in large urban centers and yearn for the hills and valleys of home.

"I like it better here," said a young Negro girl who had moved north and then returned to the South to stay with relatives. "Up there you can go more places and do more things, but nobody cares whether you live or die. Down here, at least when I walk down the street everyone knows me. I have somebody to speak to."

Sometimes, even in the North, when the father finds good employment he may decide not to move his family. One father returned to attend the graduation of his daughter. He brought her an expensive gift. "I would take her back with me," he said, "but it's no better there."

Today the Negro is struggling to alter his way of life. Just as the children are struggling in a "state of marginality"—crossing over from one way of life to another—so the family is undergoing a similar change. I see this in my relationships with the parents.

Not long ago, a Negro father came to the school to inquire about the progress of his children. This does not happen often. Nearly always it is the mother who comes. But this father said, "When I was a boy in Alabama, I used to dream of going to school. If I had had these opportunities, I believe I could have done almost anything." He seemed so proud to be "checking" on his children. He told me to tell their teachers that he was ready to help in any way and he wanted to be notified if the children "got out of line." He said, "I want *my* children to have an education, and I am ready to make any sacrifice to see that they get it."

I once heard Mrs. Rheable M. Edwards, a Negro educator who has worked for years with hundreds of Negro families in Boston, say: "This father is a very real and important person. Unless we can get him where he can support his family, we are missing the boat completely. Many of the other family problems will disappear when the Negro man has a good job." Mrs. Edwards is right. As the father begins to think well of himself, the whole family situation changes. The children have better clothing and the proper food. A greater effort is made to see that children attend school and Sunday School and participate in community activities. The children are happier and the mother is freed of some of the burdens of the family.

There is one other factor in the complicated, present-day racial turmoil as it affects the Negro family. A "rift" has grown up between the "old Negro" and the "new, young Negro" within the same family. The old Negro is having to learn to adjust to the boldness of the young, and get used to the new ways and the new rights. It is not always easy after nearly a lifetime spent in different patterns. The new Negro is giving the old the courage to get into the fight, but at times the younger members of the family are impatient and the older ones feel that they are not needed or appreciated. This is perhaps a pattern in family relations all over the country, in white homes as well, but it seems to be more evident in Negro homes. Maybe it is because the issues involved necessitate drastic change in attitudes and manner of living.

"If it had not been for us," an old Negro man told me, "these young ones would not think so well of themselves. They laugh at us and say we are the kind who will try to talk and negotiate. They say that won't help."

And another: "These young ones have not had to go through what we did. They have had everything on a silver platter. We're afraid they might not appreciate all this freedom."

The older Negro accepted segregation long ago as an inevitable part of life. He has not known anything else. Yet a yearning for freedom in its true sense, for self-expression and the everyday comforts, has always smoldered in him and is now rekindled in the hope that it will be fulfilled in his children. Because he belongs to another age, the older Negro has a different approach to these man-made problems. But he has an important place in this social revolution. He is needed by the "new, young Negro" in the days ahead to provide balance and perspective. He has bonds with the white man that go deeper than many of the "new young Negroes" will ever understand. It is said that because of these bonds, integration, when it is finally achieved in the South, will be of a more lasting nature than in the North.

Olivia, the old grandmother, understood this. She will never go into the streets to demonstrate, and perhaps does not even feel that she has a right to vote (a feeling many of the old Negroes have), but no one can say that she has not shown courage. It was Olivia, the grandmother—not the mother—who came to school to see about Jodie in the first days of desegregation. She said, "This wasn't no idea of mine—us coming down here. But they said it's the law now. We don't want any more trouble—just peace and what's coming to us . . ."

Jodie did "come through." Day by day I saw Olivia's influence on him. Olivia kept his shirts washed and ironed. She always had a few coins hidden away in a bowl when Jodie needed something extra for school. She made sure that he didn't stay out of school, and she kept in touch with the teachers about his studies. It was Olivia who "put on her hat" and came to the PTA meetings.

On the night of graduation Olivia was there with the family. They had come from far and near to attend. The younger members of the family helped her to her seat in the balcony. For once, she didn't wear a hat. Her white hair was plaited tightly around her head, and held together with large, old-fashioned hairpins. She wore a light blue dress and had a long white shawl around her shoulders.

Jodie was the first of her family to be graduated from high school. It was a night to behold.

Jodie's name was called, and he walked up the aisle and across the stage to receive his diploma. She sat like some matriarch of old, poised in her happiness as all of her life she had been steeled to sorrow. Then the ceremony was over. Hundreds of people filed out the doors. I happened to be standing nearby, and she reached out in the crowd and placed her hand on my arm, and said softly, "If you ever need me, the night will never be too dark."

In spite of all handicaps, today's Negro children struggle for the opportunity to learn. Surely no one who has seen the human drama of the desegregation of a Southern school could question that these children are pioneers in twentieth-century America.

3

Tender Pioneers

OF all the children who came to us that first year, it was Victoria who stole my pedagogic heart. She was the first of the Negro children I came to know well; and I was brought close to her under such terrifying circumstances that a bond was formed between us which carries over to this day. I am sure I was able to teach her little, because the atmosphere at that time was not exactly conducive to wholesome learning. But from her I learned much. And there is one day in particular I shall never forget.

Victoria sat in the back of the auditorium, which was used as a study hall. That day there were some hundred and fifty white students in the room. Victoria was the only Negro, as I remember. It was a day in December in the first year, just before the school was closed the second time. Tension was so high among the students that it would have taken a policeman to maintain order. Without my knowledge, Victoria was persecuted with abusive language in whispered tones. I realized something had happened when I saw her leave the room, and spontaneously the students applauded as if they had scored a victory.

That night I couldn't sleep. How could I call myself a

teacher when a child who was under my supervision—any child—had been persecuted? I called her at her home. It was with reticence that she related the events which had caused her to leave. Victoria told me that the white students around her had whispered filthy names. "I could take that," she said. "But they kept on, and one boy looked like he was going to touch me, so I left." I told her how ashamed I was for all of us. She answered, "I understand. I don't want to cause no trouble."

The next day I felt duty-bound to explain to my students the fundamentals of American citizenship and constitutional law. We talked about the fact that no person has a right to bring harm to another. We discussed John Donne's famous line: "No man is an island, entire of itself," and the Golden Rule. I tried to think of all the things I had ever read or learned about our American heritage, so that I might in some way help these young people to understand that there could be no freedom under anarchy and mob rule.

Some were moved. They apologized; they said they were sorry they had cheered when Victoria left; they didn't know why they had, they just didn't think. And some, young boys and girls in their teens, looked at me with blood in their eyes, and whispered, "Nigger-lover."

At the end of the period, a stranger—I remember only that she wore a white dress—stood in the corridor and met the students as they came out of the room. Evidently she had been listening to our discussion. "You don't have to pay any attention to your teacher," I heard her say to some of the students. "There's another kind of law she don't know about."

I walked over to her. "Are any of these your children?" I asked. She replied, "No." I have forgotten her face, but I shall always remember her words, "There's another kind of law."

With my colleagues I saw this other kind of law and came to realize the terrible power the organized few can have upon our democratic public-school system, and upon the children, both black and white. I talked to Victoria toward the end of the first year after that dreadful incident in the auditorium. The atmosphere, we thought, was calmer then. We could talk about the things we should have done and didn't. "Victoria," I asked her, thinking at the time that the worst that could happen had, "would you go through it all again?"

She weighed her answer carefully. Finally she said, "I don't know."

"Do you think what you have gone through is really worth it?" I asked.

"I don't know," she said, "I've thought about it a lot."

There was a faraway look in her eyes, as of an old woman who had seen many sorrows. I suppose she remembered the way they had looked at her, and the things they said; and the times she climbed the hill in the rain to go home for lunch because she did not dare enter the lunchroom; and the times she wanted a drink of water at the fountain, but never quite got it.

Then she said, "The only thing I know is maybe it will be easier for someone else." There were tears in her eyes.

Because of my relationships with students like Victoria, and with many others, and because of what I have seen through their eyes, I do not believe anyone can know for certain how deeply many of the Negro children are

59

affected by the tense, unfriendly situations they have been thrust into in newly desegregated schools. Only they can say what really happens to them. I have kept in touch with many of the first Negro students who experienced one to two years of this atmosphere of violence and turmoil. It seems to me that they bear deep scars which are not likely to disappear for a long time. No doubt these harsh experiences have different effects on each child. Each has a different makeup, his own outlook on his life, a particular family background. How the children are affected depends also upon the conditions under which the school is desegregated, and the general atmosphere of tolerance or intolerance that has been building up in the community over the years.

Where there has been careful planning for desegregation and everyone in the community participates and has accepted the change, the process appears to be fairly smooth. Another deciding factor is the age at which children enter a desegregated school. There is less difficulty when they start school together than when they are first thrown together in the adolescent years, when tensions are high anyway. And by that time the children of both races have formed many prejudices and wrong impressions.

When a Negro child enters a school where he knows he is not wanted, in the midst of violence and disorder in the community and in the school, as has been the case in much of the South, he has to cope with almost unimaginable fears and anxieties. Most immediately he fears for his physical safety. This fear is well grounded. He knows that even his parents are afraid; they have expressed their fears and talked about the dangers involved if he enters the white school. I knew Negro parents who chose to send their children to segregated Negro schools for several years after the Clinton High School was opened to Negroes, because they preferred not to have them exposed to these tensions. Some Negro families moved from the state for that reason.

A Negro family may be torn within itself as to whether the children should go into the white schools under such adverse circumstances. Olivia had said, "Mary Lee [Jodie's mother] didn't want Jodie to come down here. She said there'd be trouble. But I said, 'Now, Mary Lee, you just listen to me. I know these white folks. I know the good in them and the bad too. And I just said these children deserve a chance like you know we never had; and if we have to go this way, we'll just have to go.' "

The children, then, start out from home in a state of anxiety. They have heard the discussions at home and they know there is good reason to anticipate trouble. In an atmosphere of violence, Negro children entering white schools are not only humiliated and embarrassed but they face physical danger in coming from their homes to the school building. The crowds who lined the streets of Clinton to spew their venom on our children as they walked to school each morning had their counterparts in Little Rock and countless other places in the South. Anyone who saw the expressions on the faces of these people who milled around the school, and heard the abusive language they used, could not doubt that the children were indeed in danger.

The children expressed their fears to anyone who talked to them. They described the short journey from home to school as the longest of their lives. They tried to appear brave and grown-up, but they did not know when the people who had come to jeer at them would carry out their threats. After a few days they came to look upon merely getting inside the school building as a victory. They said it was like a shelter to them. Their tense expressions relaxed a little when they got inside the school, although even there they experienced hostility.

Although the main difficulties inside the school were instigated by a very small group of white students, nevertheless these students were able to make life for the Negro children extremely unpleasant for some time. The threats and insults directed at these youngsters were enough to keep them and their teachers on constant guard for their physical safety. Such threats as: "If you come back to school, I'll cut your guts out," could be heard in the halls all through the first year. The Negro children had eggs smashed on their books, ink smeared on their clothes in the lockers, knives flourished in their presence, nails tossed in their faces, and spikes left on their seats. Obscene words were constantly whispered in their ears.

There were many instances of harassment and persecution which we will never know about. In my talks with Negro girls I learned that they cut too deep for words. Listen to the Negro children:

"They make faces at us."

"They call me 'Liza'—what you reckon they call me Liza for? That ain't my name."

"One boy carries an ice pick—always showin' it to me."

"One boy twisted a piece of rope like a noose and stick his finger in it like it was my head."

"I hate that school and everything in it. Every morning I think I can't go back there. I'm trying to keep my mind on what I have to do—make something of myself."

Where this "other kind of law" has taken over, the

Negro children learn to expect the worst. Because they are afraid, they devise not always wise means of self-protection. Although the carrying of knives is prohibited, it is hard even today to find a Negro boy who does not own a small pocket knife. And in dangerous times these children rally toward their natural leaders, who act as their protectors, or at least try to. One day some white boys crowded a small black boy against his locker in the hallway. They were making some sort of game of frightening him. The child stood shaking—and then a tall Negro boy pushed his way through the semicircle. "Don't you touch him," he said. And a fight broke out between the white boys and the older Negro boy. Such incidents are common in times of racial turmoil. Teachers and the students are all under great strain, never knowing exactly when a conflict will flare up.

The Negro youngsters do not seem to forget who among the white children were antagonistic and who were kind. A Negro girl said years afterward, "I will always remember John [a white boy], who told the other students to leave me alone." Or they will say, "He was the only one who was not afraid to speak to me. I will always like him for that." They remember all the little things that are such very big things in any adolescent's life. I don't believe Laurie will ever forget how she was treated.

Laurie was a neat, mannerly, intelligent girl. In an all-Negro school she would no doubt have been a leader and very popular. She came from a good home; her people were aristocrats among the Negroes, and she had been brought up more carefully than many white children I have taught. To my knowledge, during the two years she was in our school (the first two years of desegregation), no one ever spoke to her and she never participated in a school activity outside of routine classwork.

Some days, as she went about her work, I would look at her and wonder what it would be like to sit a whole year in a class and not have anyone except the teacher speak to me. I wondered what it would be like not to have anyone you could ask for a sheet of paper or a pencil. And what it would be like to have a new dress, and not a single person say, "How pretty you look."

Laurie sat in the front row in the class. Whenever there were flowers on my desk, she would reach out and touch them gently with her long, slender fingers; and frequently she would change the position of a jonquil or a tulip. And always she improved the arrangement.

One day Laurie said, "I've decided to be a teacher, but I want to work with small children." She did go on to college, but then she was married and did not teach. Her husband had a skilled job and was well prepared to take care of her. Laurie has her own family now and lives in another town. Sometimes when she comes home she visits me. It is not in her nature to harbor resentments; but when we talk about her high-school days, she does not mention happy times, as most students do. Really, there were none for her. She was robbed of days which should have been among the happiest in her life—days to which all children are entitled. And there is a sadness about Laurie, even today; perhaps it is simply the realization of what man can do to man if he wants to.

This realization is a shocking thing for children. Victoria said, years later, of her experiences: "The thing that I think now affected me the most was not the physical danger, because you get to the point that you had just about as soon die; but it was the realization of how much people could hate us. I never realized before that people could hate us as they do."

Another youngster, whom I shall call Marie, was nine years old when dynamite was thrown into her house in the late hours of the night. Off and on for weeks there had been explosions in the Negro community, so that they had become almost commonplace. Later it was said that these explosions were part of a "conditioning process" that was to culminate in the school's being blown to pieces. The explosions would come at the most unexpected times, usually late in the evening or in the early morning hours. We could feel the tremors in our own homes across town, and I always thought of the Negro children in my classes. Did they still have their arms and legs? Could they still see? And why weren't the people who committed such terrible acts apprehended? Years later, when I worked with Marie, I could see the effects on her of that horrible night.

"I was asleep when it happened," she said. "It pretty well wrecked our house. I rushed out of bed and ran to my mother. There were cars outside all up and down the road. People were excited. I looked out. There were only strange faces. All I could think was: Why would they do this to me?

"My mother always told us that white people were friendly. She said that if we got sick, or ran out of food, white people would help us. I couldn't understand. If they were like she said, then why would they want to kill us? Why? For a long time then I hated white people . . .

"Sometimes when the teacher asks who knows the answer to a question, and a white student raises his hand first, I'm afraid to raise my hand. I know the answer, but

65

something keeps me from raising my hand. I think back to why? It's always: Why?"

The realization of the evil men are capable of can change the Negro child's attitude toward white people. For down deep inside, everyone wants to be loved. And, as with any children, once these attitudes of hatred are formed, the road back to a more normal outlook is very difficult. Thus, many Negro children learn not only how much they are hated but also how to hate white people. It is a natural reaction. The children are not old enough or experienced enough in human relations to cope with the violent conditions to which they are exposed.

In this atmosphere the Negro children find studying and learning in school difficult. The ones I know showed it in their grades and in achievement tests. One day I talked to a Negro girl about college-entrance requirements. There was a failure on her record, or rather she had chosen not to complete a course and had received a failing grade. She said, "I could have passed that course, only I was so upset. You know how it was." I too think she could have passed the course under normal circumstances. In fact, she did well in much more difficult courses in college.

Even after overt violence has abated—and these incidents usually run their course within the first year—the Negro child faces other, subtler forms of harassment. Getting into the school is really only the beginning.

It is after the first year or so that we begin to see how the Negro children are affected by a "caste system," a "way of life," a "social order"—whatever you want to call it. Of course, it was there all the time—the real reason for the conflict—but it did not draw our attention or the children's because of the turbulence of the initial period of adjustment. It is that something in us all in the South that reaches down to the Negro child and dictates to him before he is old enough to know any different: "You are a Negro. You don't belong here. Can't you see you are an intruder? Why did you have to come?" This indefinible something culminates in crippling and often crushing the spirit of the child. It has already taken its toll on the parents, but he has not recognized it clearly until now. This is the real "killer of the dream." The child throws up a whole network of defenses in an effort to cope with it. And he grows to fear it deeply and keenly because now he sees and feels it in its stark reality. Before, he had just heard about it. He knew it was there, but it hadn't really happened to him. Now he is going to have to face it, and alone.

This "system" comes to bear upon him in the form of resentments, prejudices, hatreds that assume subtle forms— sly remarks and glances, people pretending he is not there. He learns now that there are other ways to show hate and prejudices than with violence and harsh words. Sometimes I have even thought the latter is almost a kinder way, because it is in the open. So often the older Negro students have said, "I see now what I have to face." This is what they are referring to. It is a difficult thing to cope with in working with Negro children. You see it too. You know it is wrong. You even feel responsible for it because you know you are a part of the South and the social order which has produced it.

A teacher can rebuke students who mistreat a Negro child openly. If a fight breaks out, you can go into the corridor and separate the children and stop the fight. But the more subtle harassment is not so easily detected or stopped. You can see the effects it has on the children; you watch them struggle to adjust to this order, and you try to change it. You see how difficult the change is going to be for everybody and how long it is going to take, so that in a sense the Negro child of today is giving up some part of his childhood to bring about a social change.

The struggle produces in the Negro child an anxiety, a deep fear which seems to be ever present. It is revealed in such questions as:

"Will I be able to play ball with the white boys?"

"Will there be a place for me when the class goes on an overnight field trip? Where will I eat and sleep?"

"Will there be someone who will walk down the aisle with me on graduation night?"

"What would happen if I sat down at the table with white students?"

It is a kind of apprehension that makes the child wonder who he is and why. For, above all else, a child desires to be accepted by those around him. The Negro boy or girl worries about being accepted in the white school by the other students and by those in authority. He comes in frightened and insecure, concerned not only for his physical safety—will he be treated kindly?—but by something else which goes very deep: his need to be wanted and loved. And he knows, as do all children, who cares about his well-being and who does not.

Very likely, the Negro child is gregarious. He has been reared in a large family and in a crowded community. He is accustomed to groups of people. When he enters a place where he is not accepted by the group and is ignored, as is the case in so many white schools in the South today, he experiences loneliness. Negro students have told me that this "feeling of loneliness" they have in the new school is so overwhelming it affects everything they do.

"Do you know what it is not to be wanted?" they say. "What it is like to hear the other children talking about parties and proms and know they're just hoping you will say you don't care to go?"

One morning a Negro girl left this poem on my desk. It was titled, "Alone."

> *I am alone;*
> *The place is dark*
> *No sign of day*
> *No sound of lark.*
>
> *No kids are here to play with*
> *No place here to walk to*
> *No one here to stay with*
> *No one here to talk to.*
>
> *This place is dark*
> *I am filled with dread*
> *You see, I am alone,*
> *I am dead.*

Shortly afterwards she quit school.

Because these children feel such loneliness, they stay together, seeking refuge in each other's company. They tend to "resegregate" themselves in the white school. They feel more comfortable with each other; they ask to be together in classes. Very often teachers request that at least two Negro students be placed in the same class, never one alone, because the Negro child alone in a class of white students feels so insecure. For the same reason, Negro children tend to stay with each other during lunch and free periods, and at all social events. Resegregation in the desegregated school is very common. Negro parents are aware of this and many encourage their children to get out and mingle with the white students and take part in their activities. But this is not easy to do unless one is asked and made to feel welcome.

True, some Negro youngsters associate with white students. These are usually youngsters with outgoing personalities, youngsters with outstanding capabilities, who come from better Negro homes and are able to move about comfortably among the white students. But even here there is a point beyond which the social order dictates: "You are white. You are black." A Negro boy expressed it this way: "Some white students are friendly, but when they are in a crowd they don't want to have anything to do with me; and certainly they would never invite me to their homes."

Not long ago I asked fourteen Negro students now in school, "Do you think attending a desegrated school has been helpful to you?" Four of the fourteen said that they would prefer to go to a Negro school. I knew that in the first years of desegregation Negro youngsters had returned to their own school because they were unhappy; but I was surprised to find this many even now who would want to go back to a segregated school. "The desegregated school helps you to get along with other races," a ninth-grade Negro boy said, "but I had rather go to an all-Negro school because you feel more at home there and have more rights."

The four students who would prefer to attend a segregated school are in the ninth and tenth grades. Youngsters in the upper grades, who have come through the period of adjustment and have had a degree of acceptance, seem for the most part to have a different attitude toward a desegregated school. Here are some of their answers to the question, "Do you think attending a desegregated school has been helpful to you?"

"Yes, it has helped because you meet different people and make new friends and you learn to get along with other people in the world. When I first started to the white school, I did not like the students, but I soon learned that I had to go there for four years, so I knew I had to make friends with some of the students. Then after the first year went by, everything has worked out just fine. I think it has helped me."

"It has helped me to learn how to treat other races. It has shown me the attitude that some whites have toward the Negroes. I like the teachers and some of the students but for those who call us 'niggers' and everything else I don't think it's right."

"Yes, because it shows me how nice some people are, and how some people treat you bad. But so far I have been treated very nice. And I appreciate it."

"Yes, because it shows that you can get along with people if you want to, and settle your problems very easily."

A trained psychologist no doubt could read many implications into these statements. We can all see, however, that the Negro youngsters are greatly preoccupied with being accepted by the white students and with learning to live in an integrated school. Too, the Negro is having to learn to change his attitudes toward the white people, for he also brings to the new school suspicions and doubts about the white man and a lack of trust in him. At this point in their lives, making friends and being able to identify with white students is more important to these children than anything else in the new school. Certainly, their success in school seems to hinge largely upon this.

In group discussions with Negro students we have also talked about the specific experiences in the desegregated school which the youngsters feel have been most helpful to them. Although the Negro children express appreciation for the opportunity of having new courses and the higher standards of a desegregated school, they place "learning to get along with others" and their "contacts with other students" as the most important experiences. The relationship with the other students seems to be so essential in an adolescent's world that his staying in school often depends upon it. If the Negro child is able to make even a few friends in the new school, and comes to feel even a small part of the main group, the adjustment is much easier and he seems happier. He can endure much more from the outside if he has a few friends his own age in the school and a teacher or two to help him. At the same time, he can endure so much more "inside the school" if he has love and security at home.

"Being accepted by the group," for the Negro child, does not seem to mean the same thing as for the white child. The Negro does not expect social fraternization in the sense that white children associate with each other and extend their relationships to their lives outside school. He does not expect to hold offices in the school or be popular, although, of course, he would like to. He feels accepted if he is not treated harshly, if there are a few boys and girls who speak to him and treat him kindly.

The Negro child struggles for acceptance and recognition in various ways. In group sessions I have asked: "What is it you feel you want most in the desegregated school?" Invariably they answer, "We want to show the other children what *we* can do." The Negro youngster has something to offer, and what he has to offer is being suppressed. Perhaps it is no more than a song, but this song to him may be more meaningful, for the time being, than a recitation from Shakespeare. And this song, which he wants to bring to others, for all we know, may be nearer the true heart of music than any offered by the most tutored of the tutored.

Those who are outstanding in athletics are among the most fortunate; we seem to have accepted the Negro in sports much more so than in other activities. Those whose talents lean to "entertaining" are also accepted to some degree for what they have to give. Many Negro youngsters who have had some success in these fields come to rely upon them. Yet this may not be where their real talents or ambitions lie. But they are, however, where it is easiest to break through barriers. The Negro children know this. Boys have told me that they are going out for basketball or football just for this reason. A basketball or a football team, a school chorus or band, will always seem more truly integrated than a classroom. Here there is "team play" and everybody is a part of the team, and success depends upon everyone carrying his load and working together.

The youngster who is outstanding in his classwork also seems to be more readily accepted. White boys and girls will study with him, talk with him, and even confer honors upon him. These, however, are the exceptions.

In addition to all the fears and anxieties connected with getting to the new school, adjusting to it, and being accepted by white students, the Negro child is subjected to still another pressure. That is the pressure to achieve. Most children today are under pressure to do better and better in their studies; but the Negro child is under a very different type of stress. The white man has said, "Let's see now if you can do this." The older black man has said, "If you don't, we won't have a chance." The child feels this stress put upon him from all sides. He knows he is on trial. He knows that he must not only pass his courses but perform outstandingly if he is to get anywhere. And for the majority of them, with a poor academic background to hamper them, this is very difficult.

One of the most important factors in achievement in school is the lack of fear and the ease with which a youngster is able to assert himself and enter into the competition. Few people stop to consider what the Negro child has to go through to do well in the new situation—even his own parents. Negro youngsters react in various ways to the pressure to achieve. Some overwork themselves. Marie, for example, said, "I studied twelve hours for that examination, and to think I made a 'B.' Mother said to just study thirteen hours the next time; and I will, too, if it takes it."

Some, less endowed than Marie, do so much and then they look for a way out. Many give up and quit school. Others develop a sense of hopelessness.

"This drive to move ahead and make something of ourselves is a powerful force," Marie said. "We know that in everything we do we have got to be the best . . . You know, my grandmother never learned to read, but she could count a little. My mother only got to the fourth grade. When I started studying algebra, she tried to study with me. I saw she could have learned it if she had had a chance. My father never got to high school, but he has a brilliant mind in mechanics. I know that now. My grandmother says I'm the first of her grandchildren to come through high school. You see how important this is to me?"

I watched her wipe the perspiration from her hands that day we talked. I wondered if this generation of Negro children would ever know real peace of mind. Or what it means to sit one summer day on a cool river bank and just dream; children need time to dream. Or would they, all their lives, be occupied with claiming their place in the world?

So much of the Negro child's mental energy is spent in meeting the new conditions and in providing defenses to survive in them that he doesn't seem to have time to explore and discover in this new way of life as he should. It has always concerned me that the Negro children with whom I work do not have hobbies. I'm sure they do have some, but not to the extent that so many white children do. I rarely talk to a Negro boy who "collects things"; or to a girl who has some constructive and consuming interest outside class-work.

I have noticed also that the Negro youngsters who are moving on, especially the more intelligent ones, seem to feel a great urgency about everything. They rush in and they rush out. Time is at a premium. They have so much to make up to get on an equal footing with other children with whom they now must compete. They are keenly aware of their shortcomings in the new situation, and they work desperately to improve themselves.

The ones who possess qualities of leadership are restless. They are more sensitive to their surroundings and their lack of opportunities. Everything in them seems to cry out for self-expression, and if this self-expression is suppressed, they become very unhappy. These children have a greater sense of self-identity than other Negro children. And when this "ego," this sense of self-importance, goes unnourished or is shattered, they are miserable. These youngsters have abilities; they have a great deal to give to the world. If their ambitions are thwarted or misdirected, they may come back to us in ways we never dreamed of.

The more talented children are deeply sensitive to conditions about them, and often they appear to have a lower breaking point. They are reasonable, but they are also less patient than the others. One day two Negro girls brought Annie to my office. They had found her in the washroom crying as if her heart would break. "I can't take any more," she screamed as they helped her in. "I've had all I can take."

The girls then explained what had happened. It was a trivial racial incident—that is, compared to others we had experienced. A white girl had said to her friend in the room that she didn't like the idea of "washing her hands in the same lavatory as a 'nigger.'"

Annie was one of the most immaculately dressed, well-mannered girls in the school. She was talented in music, but she had never had an opportunity to display her talents publicly. She had tried very hard the two years she had been in the school to do everything "just right." I knew that Annie had turned away and pretended not to notice insults much worse than this. She had always been able to reason that the people who make such remarks are ill-bred and not worth bothering with. But that day the small, mean words apparently were the last straw. For Annie, the unprovoked slur was the supreme humiliation.

The girls who had brought her to my office helped her to a chair and left. She slumped over and put her head on my desk. I felt her tears on my arm. They were the same as the tears of my own children. At last, she could cry no more. She raised her head. Her young, soft face was grieved and old. She asked, "What is there for me?"

If a Negro child has physical or emotional problems, or unusual home problems, these may be intensified when he comes to the new, difficult situation. His anxieties are increased by the added tension, and the adjustment becomes all the more difficult. I have seen children with serious nervous disorders thrown into tense situations which even in the best of circumstances they could not cope with. One girl returned to the segregated school because her asthma attacks became much worse the year she was in the integrated school. Sometimes these children, under severe emotional strain, imagine things. One girl thought people were getting ready to throw pencils at her. She was very tense in class, and at times she would jump up and run to the teacher or out of the classroom. Some of the children imagine that the white boys and girls are looking at them as if they are planning to hurt them, or that they are talking about them. They fasten onto these feelings and use them as "excuses." A Negro boy who had undergone speech therapy as a child and had the condition under control found that his speech problem had become severe again in the new situation. Some youngsters become very shy and withdraw from the other students.

I relate these isolated incidents to show that in an atmosphere of tension and fear where unusual adjustments are necessary—and such an atmosphere is present to some degree in almost every desegregated situation in the South today—the seeds are there for serious mental disturbances in Negro children.

Negro children are also very sensitive to racial discord all over the country. The turmoil and dissention generate mental anguish and confusion in them. Whenever there is trouble, they seem to feel that they should be there helping. They write up petitions, letters, or express a desire to go and help. Even if they are getting along well in their particular situation, every day they see pictures and hear news of racial violence in America. On television they see Negro children taunting law-enforcement officers, having water hoses turned on them, being beaten, prodded, and dragged into police cars; and praying on church steps. Who can say what deep impressions these scenes make upon young people?

I saw how deeply the children I work with were affected by the death of the four Negro girls in the Birmingham church. "I was sick that day," said a Negro boy. "I was angry, too. I felt as if someone had done something directly to me—not to my race, but to me as an individual." "It hurts," another one said. "Any one of those girls could have been my sister. Don't you think I don't know that?"

"Well, I don't worry so much about myself," a young girl added. "I worry about my relatives in Alabama. I always think: what if it had been my father they dragged down the street?"

"I didn't think of this as a racial problem," a boy said. "I just thought how horrible it was that one human being would want to kill another—and in a church."

Each Negro child strives in his own way to adjust to the change, to be recognized and accepted, and to realize his ambitions. His struggle is hard, and real, and often painful. As with all children, some are weak and some are strong; some are better prepared to face the rebuffs and the hostilities, as well as the wonderful opportunities. No doubt, many of today's Negro children will return to the subservience of their parents, as many already have. In my own school, the drop-out rate for Negro students the first year was fifty percent. It has decreased steadily each year since. But the drop-out rate for Negro students is still twice that of the white students. And the drop-out rate for Negro boys is twice that of the Negro girls.

A few years ago I had occasion to hear some of the Negro young people of the first desegregated class discuss their feelings. They agreed that, except for making the way possible for others, for which they seemed proud, the ordeal was of little benefit to them personally. "But, oh," one girl did say, "I wish I had held on and finished school." She had tried to take courses by correspondence but had to give up there too because she could not get a job to pay for the instruction. As she told her story, her own little girl played around the dirty, broken-down chair she sat in. "I guess I really quit because I didn't have the money to buy a gym suit," she continued. "The teacher offered me one, but I didn't want charity. Seems silly now."

Many of these children are deeply hurt in the process of attending a desegregated school that is not properly prepared for them and in which there is a hostile atmosphere. But perhaps the vast majority of them are hurt no more, or not even as much, as they would be if they were left to a life in which all men are not free. The Negro has everything to gain and little to lose. In this spirit, one Negro mother advised her son: "You just learn how to get along with those white folks down there. There ain't nothing worse they could do to us than they have already done."

Another Negro child was afraid to come to the white school and asked her mother, "What will I do if one [meaning a white student] sits by me?" Her mother replied, "Honey, they'se people just like us."

79

4

The Hardest Lessons

To recount the ordeals of the Negro children in the process of desegregation and not relate the trials of the white children would be misleading. Together they are trying to reconcile an unjust heritage, and their struggle is manifested in a hundred ways.

Of course, most of the white children would not have agreed with the Negro mother who told her child, "They'se people just like us." The average white youngster in the South conceives of himself as superior to the Negro. He comes by this feeling so innocently that he does not even realize it is a part of him. Everything to which he has been exposed sanctions the doctrine of racial superiority. The statutes of the South directing separation of Negroes and whites in railway cars, theaters, restaurants, parks, playgrounds, schools have made separation seem proper. In other words, the laws in themselves have not only implied but legalized "superiority."

And just as the Negro child has absorbed the feeling of inferiority which society has imposed upon him, so the white child enjoys a self-assurance, an inherent sense that his proper place is "up front." Even the poorest white child has not had to cope with the problems of statutory discrimination experienced by the Negro, nor has he had to struggle to realize his basic constitutional rights. His parents have never been turned away from a church, a school, a voting booth. So there is a vast difference between being "poor white" and being "poor black."

The white child, then, holds the old values which are deeply entrenched in his environment. He holds these values in earnestness and sincerity. The past has been pictured as so beautiful and comfortable that it is painful for him to think it otherwise. To his way of thinking, it even becomes morally wrong to do so. He has been reared to believe that things are all right as they are.

These children have been little exposed to discussions on the problems of the Negro in America. One white boy was asked as he got off the school bus one morning in 1956, "How do you feel about going to school with Negroes?" His reply was typical: "I never thought anything about it before. Nobody ever talked to me about it." I could certainly understand the boy's statement because, in a sense, I felt the same way. I recalled that I had been through two state universities and taken any number of education courses and never once can I remember that a professor mentioned the remote possibility that one day those of us in training to be teachers would have Negro children in our classes. Our society has been so stagnant that the majority of these children have not been reared to consider that one day they might have to adjust their patterns of living to cultures other than their own. We notice this same condition in working with white children in the mountains, where they are taught little of other people, where in-breeding is common, and all outsiders and people who are different in any way are looked on with suspicion. There are many small communities in the east Kentucky and Tennessee mountains where a Negro, or an Indian, has never been permitted to live. The people pride themselves on having no racial problems. They boast that they solve the problem by keeping the outsiders out— never feeling any responsibility for them, or considering the fact that they have to live somewhere.

One might think that children who have never been in a position to question the old way of life, or the old values, would now accept the new with the same lack of questioning. To some extent, they do. Yet we see the smoldering attitudes come to the surface, and we see how deeply engrained these attitudes are and how innocently the young white children have absorbed them as a basic part of their moral values.

One cold wintry morning I was administering tests to some fifty or more students in the school library. The students were instructed to seat themselves at the large reading tables, not more than four students to a table. There was one Negro boy in the group. He went to the back of the room (as Negro children often do) and sat down at a table. No white student came to sit with him. We were crowded and there were five students at some of the tables. Everyone saw the problem. We waited, but no one offered to occupy the vacant seats at the table with James.

Then I asked two boys from a crowded table to sit with him. Reluctantly, and making a great show of it, they went. The other youngsters eyed them silently. At the first break, they returned to their friends. One of the boys, named Sam, came up to me. Sam was a tall, lanky farm boy with a ruddy complexion and a quick temper. He was sensitive, sullen, proud—so ignorant he was eloquent. He wouldn't give in to learn. He was set for trouble. He struck me as a boy who might one day kill and not feel any sense of guilt or sin.

"I just can't sit by a nigger," he said. "I just can't do it. I'm sorry. I can't help the way I feel." There was no doubt he was sincere in his feelings.

That morning I would have a long time to think about what I had seen. This was "achievement test day." It takes several hours to take achievement tests, which, along with other things, tell us a great deal about our students. From them the students too would learn many things about themselves. We would record the scores and make careful charts and graphs and study them thoroughly. But there was one thing the tests would not tell us: why no one would sit with James.

As I gave the test, I observed James with his head bowed in a world alone, yet full of people, working away as best he could. I watched the other boys, seemingly smug in their feeling of "superiority." I kept asking myself, "Where are we failing that these young people would feel toward each other in this way? What is happening inside James this moment? He has seen how they feel. What is happening inside Sam? Does he realize what such hatred can do to an individual?" I wondered what good this knowledge from books would be if in the end these youngsters couldn't communicate with each other.

Here again, as with the Negro children, the reactions of the white youngsters toward attending school with Negroes are both individual reactions and group reactions, and they are complex. The white youngster comes into the high school with well-formed attitudes toward the Negro which range all the way from complete acceptance (very rare) to a noncommittal attitude to complete hostility. All in all, the white children meet the new situation very much as they are led to by their parents and by outside influences. If the parents have set an example of genuine tolerance and understanding, if in the home high ethical and moral standards are observed, more likely than not the child will follow the parents' example, even though there is racial discord all around him. Children not only are influenced by the school, home, and community atmosphere, but they reflect it.

Generally speaking, the white youngsters desegregated in the upper grades might be divided into three main groups. And almost invariably their parents could be classified in the same way. The first group is friendly and welcomes the Negro children. They seem to be able to talk "with" and not "to" them. They don't appear to be inconvenienced in any way because Negro children are now among them. These students believe in school desegregation and they are not afraid to speak out for it. They will say it is "just and right." This group comprises so few students even in this part of the South that I am not certain it should even be called a group. Perhaps I should say there are a few scattered individuals who feel this way. I mention them here because they often furnish a nucleus of leadership in the newly desegregated school. I would not know how to estimate the number of these youngsters in the South today. In our school I knew perhaps twenty-five white children who felt this way in over eight hundred.

These children interest me particularly. Time has vindicated their position. And I feel that through them and others like them we might find answers to our racial problems. These children seem to be fairly free of deep-rooted prejudices. I've found, in my work with Negro and white youngsters over the years, that these children come from very stable home backgrounds. This does not necessarily mean great wealth, but rather security in their family relations. The parents usually have had broadening experiences such as travel—or they have come to the South from other sections of the country, or have worked or attended school with people of other races and nationalities and are acquainted with other cultures, so that their prejudices or fears of others have abated. Frequently, these are the children of professional people—lawyers, doctors, teachers, scientists, people with a higher level of education. These children come from homes where the parents engage in challenging conversations and where questions of race, religion, and sex are freely discussed. In their homes there is an "open" atmosphere where issues are talked out. The parents know and admit that we all have prejudices of one kind or another, they know that we are all different, and they accept these differences. The children are prepared in advance for differences of opinion and new experiences. They meet new situations straightforwardly and as a natural part of daily living. They can stand "on their own" and against crowds.

The second group, definitely the majority, is opposed to desegregation in principle. They don't know anything else except to be opposed to it. This is their heritage. It is as right and proper in their minds not to sanction desegregation as it is for the first group to condone it. Within this group there are varied opinions and degrees of opposition. Some seem to be able to adjust to the idea under certain conditions and to a limited extent. A white student may bring himself to accept the idea of attending a class with a Negro, but he cannot bring himself to sit next to him in class. Or he may speak to the Negro student but not walk down the hall with him. The range of opposition or disapproval is very wide. Even the limited tolerance these people may display does not extend to social activities in any form.

This group is opposed to mob rule and violence, and the mistreatment of the Negro, and especially so after they have been exposed to it. They claim to respect constitutional law, because it is a prerequisite to order in a free country, and because their parents before them claimed respect for order. As in the case of many of their teachers, they would not promote desegregation but they would not openly work against it, because it is the law. Yet in reality they have not accepted that law in "heart and spirit," even though they may say they have.

These words "law and order" provide a means for children, and adults, to ease their consciences. They serve to postpone the moral decision—the time when we must say, "This not only is legal, but it is right." In a democracy, no one can find fault in one's stand for "law and order." "Law and order" are basic to our form of government. I know from my own experiences how convenient it was to be "for law and order" as if that solved the whole problem. I know now that I had not faced the human, moral issues involved in this struggle, because of my background and the "closed society" in which I was brought up.

In this group, then, the attitude of the white children toward the Negro children is rather passive, lacking personal involvement. They seem to feel that if you don't look, or don't become involved, it will all go away and everything will be as it always was. These youngsters have perhaps been told by their parents: "We don't approve of this. We would prefer you didn't attend school with Negroes if we had a choice. But since it is the law now, we must obey the law. You don't get yourself into any trouble. You leave them alone and they will leave you alone." The white children in this category are, to my mind, the most representative of the youth of the South today. And it is in this group that the greatest change is taking place. Even though for the time being they hold a "middle ground," they are kindly people and they are hurt when a Negro child is mistreated. But their kindliness has not yet extended to seeing that the Negro child is not hurt in the first place.

During the days of violence, we saw displays of fine leadership from young people in this group. Once they were in the situation, they seemed to see beyond the noise of the mobs to the effects of anarchy—this, even though these children would not of their own choice attend school with Negroes. On one occasion, when the school was closed, the leaders in this group of youngsters made a personal appeal on their own initiative to school authorities to reopen the school. "We can make this work," white boys pleaded with officials, and offered to help in any way to ease conditions in the school. Considering the tensions in the community at that time, it took courage for these boys to say this—because even they, at that time, had not been able to bring themselves to admit publicly that it was "right" for Negro children to come into their school.

The president of the Student Council, an intelligent young man and an outstanding leader, said: "I didn't ask for integration and I wasn't enthusiastic about getting it, but the Supreme Court said that our school should be integrated, and so I thought I should do all I could to bring this court order about peacefully."

The more moderate white students were particularly effective in influencing others who might go either way, who would either keep to a "middle ground" or join the radical segregationists. A youngster can go to another youngster and say, "I don't believe in this either. I know how you feel; but we don't want trouble." The boy or girl who stands undecided will listen.

The children who took a moderate stand suffered in many ways. They felt sorry for the Negro boys and girls when they saw them in their ordeal, and they tried to be friendly. When they were, even in the most minimal ways, the more radical students who resented any form of kindness to the Negro students then exerted every effort to make them feel guilty; they were called 'nigger lovers.' At this, some white children would stop speaking to the Negro children and refuse to be seen near them; "they did not want to be involved." This change of attitude had an effect on the Negro youngsters too; they could not understand why anyone who had tried to be friendly would suddenly turn away.

After a time, some of the more moderate white students assumed a "protective role" toward the Negro children they had so often seen being mistreated. One white boy said: "When it got really bad, a bunch of us worked it out so that if we saw the Negro kids being mistreated we would not be afraid to tell the teachers. We got tired of them taking advantage of the Negro students." On occasion we saw boys take action to protect the Negro children. Football players rescued three Negro boys who had been cornered by a mob on the street. They took the Negro boys to the principal's office.

In these and other situations we saw the inward struggle of the white youngsters. A change in attitudes is an uneven, shifting process—not a sudden thing at all—but there is change, and it is coming much faster than I would have dreamed a few years ago. The white supremacists in their zeal have, I believe, done more than they will ever realize to accomplish the very thing they are fighting against. And that is to hasten the day when white and black men will see each other as equal. Many of the more moderate white children, who accepted the legal mandates and tried to live up to them, have been disillusioned beyond words at the grotesque, bizarre reasoning and the hatreds called forth in this conflict. They are beginning to decide that they do not want to be identified with these extremists. They are beginning to look deep into their own consciences—something they have not done before. And because youth is itself inquisitive, because it is a time of revolt, they begin to ponder in their own minds the things they have learned concerning the promises of democracy and Christian teachings. They begin to analyze the moral aspects of the Negro's struggle. They question the inconsistencies in our culture. They see conflicts. I have known many white students who felt so confused that they sought advice from their ministers. A white boy said one day, "I would just like to get out of the whole thing, but I'm not sure where one would go to get out of it."

While some youngsters search for answers, the white children in the third group, because of parental or outside influences, or because of their own natures, are violently opposed to attending school with Negroes. In this part of the South, in a border state, these children are a minority. They usually come from the lower social and economic strata of a community. Their parents are usually uneducated. A parent in this group said, typically: "When they let those niggers in there, I taken my boy out and he just kinda lost interest, I guess. But I've said, before I'd raise my children up with a nigger, I'd raise 'em up dumb like I am."

These are the neglected white people of the South. About the only thing they have ever had in their favor is that, because they are white, they have always been considered above the Negro. They resent the Negroes more than ever because now the Negroes offer the "poor whites" competition in the labor market and elsewhere. Often, because of poverty, ignorance, social incompetence, the children in this group have serious emotional and other problems; and, as with the Negro children, their problems are magnified by the tension of the situation. These children are accustomed to a dictatorial home atmosphere in which matters are not discussed freely; and their parents' thinking is very rigid.

The children harbor a host of prejudices and misconceptions regarding other people that are very difficult to change or modify. They have never known any other way to look at the Negro except through the uncompromising attitudes of their parents. These children enter a desegregated situation thoroughly convinced that Negroes are supposed to be servants. They quote the Bible as their proof. They believe that the Negro wants one day to take over the government and therefore he must be "kept in his place." They believe that Negroes not only are inherently inferior to white people but that they are stupid and incapable of learning. They are certain that Negroes commit crimes more readily than white people, and that all Negroes will steal, rape, and murder. Social equality to them means that the Negro wants intermarriage.

The children have been so indoctrinated with these beliefs that they refuse to consider any other possibilities. Their prejudices not only encompass the Negro but extend to Jews and Catholics, though in less virulent form.

In these children, I have seen expressions of hate and attitudes I had never seen in children before. One day I had occasion to talk at length with Sam, the boy who had reacted so violently to sitting at the same table as a Negro student for an examination. His actions by this time were openly rebellious. I left my class to talk with him. Of course, I had already seen that he felt deeply about the Negroes; but now I learned that his hatreds were so intense that there seemed to be no way I could reach him or even reason with him. He said, "If one [meaning a Negro] ever acts like he will bother me, I'll kill him." He showed me a knife he carried for this purpose. He expressed fear that he would be attacked. He explained that he felt it was no more wrong to kill a Negro than it would be to kill a rabid animal in the streets. He said, "They should be killed or sent back to Africa." He explained that his parents and his older brothers felt the same way. The only time I felt I had come anywhere close to reaching him was when we began to talk about what could happen to him, and how his life would be changed, if he did bring harm to another person. I wasn't even sure about this. Sam needed help badly; and I was desperate to know how to help him.

And Sam was not alone. There were students in this group who were, I have no doubt, hired to instigate trouble. There are newspaper accounts quoting the principal of the school as stating that some white boys admitted they had caused trouble because they had been urged to do so by adults who offered them money. One student said he had been offered $50 to "beat up a Negro boy." These students carried placards outside the school. They were part of the mobs on the streets. They organized student gangs. They met regularly and invariably were present at outbreaks and disturbances. In school they relayed whispering messages: "Make trouble—any way—just make trouble." They waged a "war of nerves" against the Negro children. The principal described their tactics in this way: "A Negro student will come out of a classroom only to be met at the door by the silent stares of a segregationist group. The Negro will walk down the hall only to be followed by the group. On other occasions a Negro may be at his locker. The group will approach the Negro with hands in pockets and say something like 'I've got a six-inch knife in my pocket.'"

These youngsters were so taken with racial turmoil that schoolwork became secondary to them. Their grades dropped, and they lost interest in their classes. Although in most cases they were backed up in their actions and attitudes by their parents, in some cases the parents were in disagreement over the issues, which made the children even more confused. Some youngsters, however, were able to see that their parents might be wrong in their feelings toward Negroes, and they were torn between the influences of their families and the influences of school and friends. I remember one girl who had been told she could not attend school with Negroes. After her father went to work, she slipped off to her classes. "My father doesn't understand," she said. "I can't get behind in my schoolwork. He doesn't realize what this can mean."

It is when the parents condone disobedience that the problem becomes especially difficult for school authorities. One day I asked a young girl in my class to remove a badge which she wore conspicuously on her blouse. These badges —"Keep Our White Schools White"—were distributed by radical segregationist leaders and were worn by students in this extreme group. They had a disturbing effect upon the Negro students, as well as on the others, and were prohibited in the school.

"If you tell me I can't wear this," she said, "I'll get my father, and when he comes up here, you'll wish the Klan had come instead."

But the significant thing is what happened to the girl during this time. She was soon ostracized by her classmates for her extreme attitude, and before the end of the year she left school, never to return. Such students are very often children who have been neglected for various reasons, and have been set apart from the mainstream. Suddenly they find in these issues a way of asserting themselves. Much to our sorrow, they are often beyond our control.

This group of youngsters is fertile prey for the youth organizations affiliated with the adult segregationist and white supremacists groups. One such organization, the White Citizens Youth Council, an affiliate of the White Citizens Council, is dedicated to the principles of racial hatred, and its program is reminiscent of Hitler's program for youth. In 1956–57 I saw a chapter in operation which affected the boys and girls I taught. We were never able to determine the exact membership, as the students themselves were in disagreement as to the number who belonged.

Their estimates ranged from 50 to 107 students. I saw this organization overnight twist the thinking of fine boys and girls. They were proud to be members. They displayed the Confederate flags and the provocative badges on their person, and carried the placards. For many of these youngsters it was the first time in their lives that they had been looked to as something important. They were made to feel important by the segregationist leaders—something we had failed to do.

The membership cards of this organization, which were later produced in court trials, contained the following pledge:

I, ——, a white citizen, believe in the separation of the races as ordained by the CREATOR, uphold racial segregation, am loyal to the United States of America, to the Constitution, and believe in the divinity of Jesus Christ.

Some of the members described it as "a sort of religious organization." They actually believed it was.

The meetings these youngsters attended were held in back rooms off alleys, on roadsides, under the guidance of radical, self-appointed leaders, some of them completely uneducated, disgruntled, unsuccessful people who certainly were no example for children. Some of these leaders were later convicted of felonies and sent to federal prisons. Some were people we had never seen before or heard of, who seemed just to "drop in" out of nowhere. These fly-by-night leaders so fascinated this group of children that the children were led to distribute leaflets of the Ku Klux Klan inside the classrooms—leaflets containing the vilest type of propaganda. This "literature" replaced the homework of these youngsters for weeks.

Their indoctrination went far beyond mere school desegregation. In fact, as time went on, these adult leaders unveiled a whole list of things they were against. One paper, entitled "The Unholy Three," expounded the dangers of fluoridated water (stating it contained rat poison); polio serum (stating it had already killed and maimed children); and mental hygiene (which was called a "subtle and diabolical plan of the enemy to transform a free and intelligent people into a cringing horde of zombies"). The leaflet ended with the admonition: "Fight communistic world government by destroying the Unholy Three. It is later than you think." This paper was imported by a group which called itself "Keep America Committee" of Los Angeles, California. All the leaflets and literature mentioned the dangers of interracial marriage or biracial sexual relations. This was the strongest argument used by the segregationists and played upon the fears of both parents and students. There was another document entitled "U.N. Wanted for Murder." I could not begin here to describe all the inflammatory literature that was placed in the hands of these children.

What did they talk about at their meetings? I asked one of the boys in my class who left such a group. He confided: "We talked about how we would hate niggers and the people who take up for them."

"Does this mean your parents and your teachers who advise you to stay out of trouble?" I asked him.

"Anybody," he said. "They're all nigger-lovers."

I asked him if his leader mapped definite plans for the members. He replied, "No, we just talked. Sat around for hours and hours. I got tired. They didn't tell us exactly what to do—just said a lot of things."

He did not have to say any more. We both knew the change which came over our students after they joined such a group. They were never quite the same. The radical segregationists saturated their minds with hatreds and misconceptions at a most vulnerable time in their lives. I am happy to say that this organization in our community disbanded before the end of the first year, apparently for lack of funds and membership. But it took its toll on many students. Many cultivated a complete disregard for the rights and property of others. We saw a carry-over of disrespect of authority of all kinds among this group of children. Some boys took to the streets and at night helped overturn cars and smear paint on public buildings. There was a sharp rise in juvenile delinquency. White students, aided by ex-students and others, smashed windows in the high-school building and helped hang dummies of Negroes in effigy.

Some of these students realized their mistake after they had become involved. Then they tried to get out. But they had already committed themselves before friends and townspeople. As the violence ran its course, and people came to realize that this type of conduct could not be tolerated, these children suffered in many ways. Other white children became afraid to have anything to do with them. They were investigated by police and government officials, taken into courts as witnesses, and referred to as "troublemakers." Their leaders, the people whom they had idolized, were rebuked publicly and in the courts. These children underwent silent humiliation. They lost their cause. Some transferred to other schools of their own accord after having been embarrassed by their actions, or because of the convictions they had acquired. Some quit school. There were those students who had been looking for an excuse to leave school. They joined the service, got married, tried to find a job. Of course, these things might have happened anyway, but one cannot but think their chances of completing their education might have been better had we not permitted such distractions.

Some stayed on. We picked up the pieces as best we could; all of us felt responsible for what happened to these children. Happily, some have been able to emerge enlightened citizens because of the experience.

Beyond the individual reactions of white children coming to a desegregated school in a time of turmoil, there are two very deep implications for our white children in the integration crisis. The first of these is that within the past decade, all over the South, there has been such mockery of the "legal" law of the land that the basic concepts of democracy are being undermined. Our children echo us: "Education? For what? The Law? Whose law? Which law?"

As the woman in white said that horrible day, "There's another kind of law." We have seen it. These children have seen it and they are still seeing it in some parts of the South. This "other kind of law" is contrary to everything this nation stands for and everything these children have been taught in school about the workings of a democracy. There are the economic boycotts, pressure upon public officials, mob violence, persecution of individuals, dynamiting of private and public property, testing of methods in our state legislatures to bypass a ruling of the Supreme Court.

Many legislators admit publicly that they have doubts about the constitutionality of the very laws for which they stand up and vote—and admit in front of today's children that they are "delaying measures." What kind of an example is this for future citizenship? Are we sufficiently concerned that what our children see us do today might come back and plague us in another way sometime in the future?

In one Southern town I visited, a large billboard at the edge of the city limits proclaimed: "Chief Justice Warren is a Communist. Get Rid of the Supreme Court." I wondered how the history and government teachers in this town reconciled their teaching with this sort of thing; and especially since the fathers of some of the students were perhaps responsible for that billboard. Under these circumstances, the child is very likely to come up with an attitude of "If I don't like something, I will just destroy it." And in the end such actions serve to break down not only the authority of the school and of the teachers, of education and law, but also the authority of the parents themselves.

The second deep implication is that where racial turmoil accompanies school desegregation it serves to weaken the public-school system of the South, and the education of white as well as Negro children is seriously affected. In communities where schools have been closed, or where it is threatened that they will be closed, many parents are meeting the crisis by sending their children to private schools to avoid having their education interrupted. Of course, there are others who are sending their children (and especially the girls) to private schools because they feel they cannot accept integration.

All over the South today private schools are booming.

No longer do they take the so-called "problem children," or only the children of the wealthy. The demand for admittance is such that they are able to be very selective. In fact, it is difficult today to get the so-called "average" child into a select private school.

In some towns private schools have been organized as "makeshift" measures. These "makeshift" schools are not always accredited; this means that they do not meet the minimum standards required by state and regional educational groups in the way of proper classroom space, adequate libraries, laboratories, and the like. Often their staffs are not properly certified to teach; and in general they have proved unsatisfactory.

Although the public schools of the South have been improved greatly in the past twenty years, many are still poorly staffed, inadequately equipped, and insufficiently housed. An alarming number of our teacher-trained graduates migrate to other parts of the nation because of low salaries, crowded classrooms, and poor working conditions in general. When a school is plagued with racial tension, obtaining adequate personnel becomes especially difficult, as experienced teachers will not come into a problem situation when they can easily do well elsewhere. Our children are the ones who suffer the most from these conditions.

The weakening of the public-school system of the South which surely is taking place where schools are disrupted by racial tension will produce a cultural gap for today's children which is almost unthinkable to true educators. Repairing the damage will take years. Negro and white children of the low-income groups will be affected the most, for these are the children whose parents cannot afford to send them to private schools. When the education of children is interrupted in this manner, the time lost in studies because of dissentions and distractions in the classrooms is almost inestimable. In Clinton I saw even into the third year of desegregation the time that the teachers, of necessity, had to take from their classes to deal with racial problems. For days on end, it seemed, the children were distracted by the turmoil about them. For two years we had to shorten the schoolday by an hour to allow for commuting time to the relocated school, and this at a time when educators all over the country have been talking of extending the schoolday. The over-all attendance at the school was five percent lower than in previous years. Tests in our school after the first years of integration indicated that the children had not achieved in their schoolwork what they should have.

Children cannot be educated properly in an atmosphere of tension and strife. The education of boys and girls is not something one can turn on and off at will. It is a continuous process, and any interruption in that process is detrimental to the child.

Those who cry the loudest, "I'd rather have my child dead or grow up ignorant than go to school with Negroes," are ironically the ones who suffer the most. Sending their children to other public schools or to private schools works for few people. In the first place, not many children are happy when they are separated from their classmates. Leaving home often presents personal and family problems; and then, of course, there is the cost involved. As a result, many drop out of school. Or they frequently fail in the new school situation and eventually return—confused and out of tune with their group.

It has been a sad experience to see parents bring their children back to school a year or two years later and hear them say, "Help me with my child. I can't do anything with him. I want him to finish school." They reach the point where they are glad to have the children back in any school. The race-baiters and the politicians don't have the answers now—nor do many teachers.

For it is difficult for the child to pick up where he left off. His pride has taken a serious beating. The attitudes of hate and disrespect for authority of all kinds that have been developed in him, and which we stood by and permitted him to develop, are carried over into every part of his life. We taught him to hate others. Now he hates himself—everything. And, as with the Negro child, the road back to normal attitudes is difficult and often can never be reached.

I have yet to talk to a student who was in our school from 1956 through 1960 who does not say his high-school career was affected. The older ones will talk about it now. "I couldn't keep my mind on my studies," a young man said who was having difficulty in college. "That was when I needed to be learning how to study."

After a while, the parents began to see it also. As one belatedly enlightened mother remarked: "My son was such a good student up until 'the trouble.' I guess it just did something to him. I couldn't see it at the time."

5

Black and White Together

AFTER desegregation becomes a reality, and tolerance re- places violence, the conditions and the problems I have described begin to disappear. We now see the white children, as well as the Negro children, under very different circumstances. The process of "integration" becomes possible.

It might be well to emphasize the difference between "desegregation" and "integration." Desegregation involves the admittance of the Negro children into the white school in compliance with the law. Integration involves the conversion of the two groups into a smooth-running organization relatively free of tensions, in which the students have good working relationships with each other. The tension and the turmoil have to be eased before the children can achieve good working relationships. Integration is a gradual process. It involves the dissolving of prejudices that cannot be affected by law. It is a personal matter, and something which must come from within the individual.

We know, of course, that the age at which Negro children enter the white schools has much to do with the ease with which a school becomes integrated. As Dr. Robert Coles of Harvard University stated in a study on the desegregation of Southern schools: "There is a vast difference between six and sixteen." Experience thus far has shown that when the children enter the first grade together the problems seem to be lessened considerably. By the time a student is ready to enter high school, usually at thirteen to fifteen years of age, so many of his basic attitudes are formed that any attempt to change them is very difficult for him. This applies to the Negro as well. To bring the two groups to the point where they work together harmoniously necessitates a concentrated effort on the part of everyone concerned. Then, too, adolescence itself is a time of high tension with special physical and social problems that constitute additional hurdles apart from the stresses of race relations.

The process of actual integration of the children involves an extremely wide range of individual reactions. For every generalization I might make concerning what happens to these children as they learn to accept each other as equal human beings, I can also think of an exception to that generalization. Generally speaking, however, integration begins to become a reality through the very fact that the children are mutually involved in attaining an education and are in daily association with each other, even though this association may be no more than sitting in the same classroom or walking down the same corridors. The contact provides them an opportunity to measure and sift their experiences with each other. As a result, there appears to be a gradual development of insight and discretion on the part of the white student as well as the Negro student.

They see their friends changing their attitudes. A white student may like the way a Negro child sings, laughs, or tells a joke. He discovers that much of what he has heard about the Negro is false. For example, youngsters sometimes have the idea that all Negroes are dirty or smell and cannot learn. A class experience contradicts this. In the same way, the Negro student may come to the new school with very set ideas about the white youngsters (he frequently does), and a class experience contradicts what he has been taught to consider an unchangeable fact.

An accumulation of such experiences begins to produce some measure of change in the individual. How much change is produced or the exact time at which it may take place is practically impossible to gauge. Individuals differ in their reactions to situations and new experiences, as do communities and regions.

In some instances, the change appears to be rather sudden, although it is doubtful that it really is. I remember an instance when a Negro student read a paper in class in which he explained how much an in-school job had contributed to his staying in school. A white boy in the class was so affected by the presentation that he appeared to change his attitude completely toward Negro students after that. He said, "I never dreamed our Negro students had to go through the things they do." But then the questions arise: Had the white boy really changed his attitudes toward Negroes as suddenly as he appeared to have done? Was this only the climax to an accumulation of experiences with fellow students? Had he been searching subconsciously for a reason to change his attitudes? Certainly the climate was set so that the white boy was receptive to admission of change.

On the other hand, some youngsters do not seem to change at all. In this same class where the Negro boy explained his ordeals of coming to school, some white students perhaps listened to his story but were not moved in the least. Such youngsters seem very comfortable in their ability to ignore the Negro students completely, just as some Negro students are content to ignore the white youngsters. In fact, I have known white students who tried to be friendly with Negro boys and girls and were met with such a cold reception that they gave up. Other white students ignore the Negro youngsters but inwardly feel guilt about it. They reconcile their actions with the attitude that "it is best this way." This attitude appears to be very prevalent not only among students but among adults as well, and even some teachers. These people say such things as: "I feel sorry for them." "I admire their courage." "I wish it did not have to be this way."

But all of this does not mean that even amid token desegregation little change is taking place, or little movement toward integration. The change is evident in individuals. And just as an accumulation of experiences can begin to change an individual, so an accumulation of changed individuals does begin to change a community and ultimately a society.

I know a white boy and a Negro boy who are now very close friends in college and study together because the white boy learned in their years in high school that the Negro boy was a strong student and a likeable person with high ideals and moral standards. The white boy learned to respect him for what he really was. One day, when the white boy came home for a visit from college, I said, "I hope you will look after Dan [the Negro boy] and see that he has friends and doesn't get homesick." He replied with a smile, "He will be the one to look after me." The amazing thing is that at one time I knew the white boy as a very prejudiced person who would have nothing to do with Negroes.

One of the remarkable and encouraging aspects of this process of integration is that a white youngster may change his attitude toward a Negro from antagonism to benevolence and tolerance—but I can't recall ever having seen the reverse. New students coming into high school from families or neighborhoods where racial prejudice is prevalent may first express some discomfort. But gradually they become reconciled to attending school with Negroes; and after a while they even begin to take pride in their progress in human relations. This provides avenues for communication. And communication leads to understanding and, ultimately, change. It is very rare that a white student hates a Negro student when he gets to know him well; and the same is true of the Negro student.

This change in individuals, largely made possible by the adult reactions in a school or a community and by insistence that young people respect law and discipline themselves, is a wonderful thing to see in young people. As they free themselves of prejudices, they even begin to look upon themselves as stronger persons. The development of more tolerant attitudes is not an isolated process, it carries over into other areas of learning. These young people appear to be emerging not only as more tolerant citizens of America but as more tolerant citizens of the world.

This change in the individual does not happen in a day or even in a year, but it is happening; and in working with white and Negro children over a long period, one can see the great progress that is being made toward a broader conception of the Negro's place in our society. The children in today's desegregated schools are in the midst of change, and indeed are helping to effect that change. Moreover, they may be providing answers every day where we have failed and our fathers before us failed.

We must consider, too, that change for young people may not really be as difficult as it would be for anyone whose ways are more firmly set, whose racial attitudes are engrained. The mother of one of our Negro students said, "Oh, I might stop by a fancy restaurant and go in there and sit down once and eat a big fine meal just to prove I could. But to tell you the truth, I really don't care anything about it. My pattern is made." Then she added: "My children have not set their pattern."

A white father expressed it another way. He said, "This [integration] is not really as hard for my children as it would be for me." Somehow, the way he said it, he seemed rather proud that it wasn't.

I sometimes think that the Negro and white children, in spite of outside appearances, have a closeness to each other which the adult cannot fathom; and they will work these things out for themselves. In fact, they are doing a pretty good job of it right now.

This mutual understanding characteristic of youth was exhibited by a group of students in a class discussion on "problems of growing up." A thin, vibrant white girl led the discussion that morning. She explained the various parts she felt she had to play in her everyday life: one as a frivolous teen-ager in school, one at home where she took on much responsibility for her family, and one on her job after school. She said that she had found it necessary to have some goal and that she felt a great drive "to make something of my life." "You can't just live," she stressed. "You can't just stay at home the rest of your life."

There were two Negro boys in this group. They sat in the back of the room. They did not contribute in any way to the discussion. They appeared to be studying their books the entire time, so that one would have thought they did not even know what had transpired. Later in the day I asked them if they had understood what the students said that morning. I asked them how they felt about the discussion. They expressed such enthusiasm that I realized they were really very much a part of all that had taken place, even though they did not say a word. One of the boys replied to my question: "We understand what they are talking about. It's like Linda says, 'You've got to do more than just live.' You've got to realize some goal—something inside you that says, 'Get out and make something of yourself.' "

"I understand what she's talking about," the other boy added. "I feel the same way. She's right. That's the way we all feel."

Another day I saw this rapport exhibited in a different way. A white boy called to Reuben, a Negro, in the corridor: "Hey, Reuben, have you got a dime? I need another dime to have enough for my lunch." And Reuben, a likable, jovial boy, reached down in his pocket and handed the other boy a dime. "Thanks," the boy said, "I'll pay you back tomorrow." Though this may seem trivial, it was really a deeply significant gesture—for both boys.

White and Negro children together have many ways of working out their problems. Actually, when they are free of adult interference or outside influence, they do meet their problems so effectively that I have often wondered whether, except for adult pressures, there would ever be any difficulty in the first place. In a peaceful atmosphere the children appear to have much more influence upon each other than we have upon them. Any teen-age group is a power unto itself. And once that group commits itself, the answers just seem to fall into place.

One way white students have of coping with racial animosities is by ignoring someone who is unkind to a Negro student. This is most effective. The white students have said, "This person just wants attention, and we just let him know that we aren't impressed. Pretty soon then, he won't bother the Negro student any more."

Although I suppose there will always be some youngsters who cannot rid themselves of their deep feelings toward Negroes, just as there are some Negroes who will not rid themselves of their feelings toward whites, the majority of white students attending desegregated schools today seem to feel a responsibility for making desegregation work, even though many are still in the process of reconciling their personal doubts.

The attitude and conduct of the Negro students during these times help greatly to determine the reaction of the white students toward them, and understandably so. The white children tend to look more favorably on those Negro students who conduct themselves properly, are clean and neat, use good language, and have good manners. Apparently, there are other considerations besides race involved here because these same white children do not associate with other white children whose dress is slovenly, who use bad language and display rough manners.

At present, one of the touchiest problems is that of social integration. When activities or clubs meet in the school and are under the supervision of teachers or school authorities, there seems to be no difficulty. But when groups meet in members' homes and have social activities outside the school, there is reluctance to include the Negro child. Swimming and dancing are the activities which cause the most concern among white adults. To date, we in Clinton have never had a student cross the color line in social dancing, although Negro children are free to come to all social activities sponsored by the school. Both Negro and white students seem to feel this is the wisest course for them to follow at this time. Certainly they have defied the predictions of the white supremacists—evidence that youth has its own way of meeting its problems.

There tends to be a natural correlation among the white children between academic achievement and response to the Negroes. Outstanding students, especially those who have experienced two to four years in a desegregated school, express friendly attitudes and concern for the Negro students in their midst. In 1959, after the school was destroyed—and one might have expected the white students to express bitterness—the class valedictorian said before the entire community: "It has been hard. It was hard on the colored students, too. We've both had a lot to bear; but because we have, we have a lot to be proud of."

Another outstanding student, when asked how she really felt about the troubles in the school now that she had been graduated, replied: "I think because we have been through the trouble we have, we are stronger. I think if we had given up, we would always have had a feeling of failure." Then she added, with the fervor of a matronly pioneer: "What I'm trying to say is, you go to church on Sunday and you hear about what a Christian should be like, and it begins not to make sense if you don't practice it during the week."

Another, who might well represent the storybook ideal of young womanhood in the South, said, "We had to learn how to use the Golden Rule."

The students I have mentioned have gone on to become responsible citizens and are leaders in their chosen fields and in their communities. One is now a college teacher. They all came from rather conventional Southern families and would never have chosen to be integrated; but when they were faced with the problem, they met it in a straightforward manner. To my mind, these children too are pioneers in twentieth-century race relations, just as the Negro children are; and they have set examples for all of us. Because they dared to speak as individuals and from their hearts, the rest became less afraid. Slowly but surely, with a kind word and a kind deed, they have made it easier for other white children to react toward Negro children as neighbors and fellow human beings.

Never was this more evident than in the sixth year that the Negro children had been in our school, still somewhat as strangers. In those six years, never once had a Negro student been called upon to participate in a public school program or even in a student assembly, no doubt largely as a result of adult fears. And it had been known to the whole school for a long time that Annie, the Negro girl whom I mentioned earlier, who was now a senior, had a beautiful voice; and even though, as I have said, she had never had a chance to perform in public. And she had never had a music lesson in her life.

And it was Christmastime.

As is the custom in our school, the members of the

Student Council, the representative student government of the school, were asked to arrange the festivities for the entire school. These were to be climaxed with a program of a serious nature.

Country boys brought greenery and straw from their fields and a huge spruce tree from the mountains nearby. The girls decorated the tree with glittering ornaments and spread the hemlock branches and the redberried holly about to provide the atmosphere of the season. They made a star of aluminum foil and placed it at the top of the tree. A cardboard box was filled with straw so that it resembled a manger, and a bedraggled doll was laid inside it.

And the students asked Annie to sing at their program.

After all this time, there were still some adults who had misgivings about a Negro singing in a public-school program. Although they claimed that "they did not mind," they felt that "others might mind." Perhaps they remembered other days too well. Perhaps they had not considered how people can change. Perhaps they had not realized that hate is not so strong in youth.

At the appointed hour, more than one thousand students marched out of the big brick building through a light sprinkle of snow and took their places on the cold bleachers in the school gymnasium. When they were seated, and all was quiet, the program began. While the school chorus stood in the background and sang Christmas carols, the wondrous story was reenacted in pantomime. First came the Wise Men from afar—clumsy boys but amazingly affecting. They approached the stable ever so slowly, so that one got the feeling of going back in time. Then, at the proper moment, Annie arose from her seat behind the piano and stepped out to the side of the Nativity scene. She began singing an old, old song, "What Child Is This?" Her voice was clear and beautiful.

The Negro children who sat in the balcony along with the white children looked down upon her proudly. "Nothing must happen to destroy Annie's song," they had said. And nothing did. Not a paper was rattled or a foot shuffled. Everyone seemed to feel: "This is Annie's moment—nothing must happen."

When the program was over and each student came forth for recognition, never, never in all the years of that school was such approval shown as when Annie stepped forth. For a moment the students held back as if spellbound, and then the applause was so deafening that chills ran down our backs and the visitors had tears in their eyes. The Negro children in the balcony relaxed and smiled contentedly.

Now the event of the year was over. The students scurried out to board the buses. Dull gray clouds hung low as if there might be more snow by night. The wind whistled lonesomely around the big brick building.

And that day Annie departed triumphantly with the others. Never, never again would she have to ask, "What is there for me?"

I was shaken with happiness, for it seemed to me that now for the first time there was real hope. One thousand boys and girls had said to a fellow student, a Negro, "You, too, are a human being. You want your chance to be what you feel you can be; and you shall have it."

In the spring of that year Annie was asked by her senior class to sing again at the graduation exercises. This was considered the highest honor they could bestow upon her. For this occasion she chose to sing "The End of a Perfect

Day." This marked another milestone for us in our long climb to better human relations. It seemed now the students wanted to do everything they could for Annie to make up for anything she might have lost. Later Annie became the first Negro saleslady to be employed by the largest department store in the area.

Today, when a Negro student succeeds, the majority of white students take pride in his success. When he is hurt, they are hurt also. Whenever there is sorrow or tragedy in one of the Negro families, the white students respond overwhelmingly. The Negro youngsters respond to their white classmates in the same way. They contribute food or money to make up baskets for needy white families at Thanksgiving and Christmas when often their own families will also be receiving baskets.

It was a cold December night last year when Amelia's house was burned to the ground. Amelia is a thirteen-year-old Negro girl who lived with her two younger sisters and her grandmother in a small cabin in "the Valley," a Negro settlement nearby. The big stove was overheated to keep out the winter winds. That night Amelia and her ten-year-old sister were asleep in an attic room. When the family was aroused, Amelia called her sister and jumped out of bed and rushed down the narrow stairway, thinking her sister was behind her. The child was perhaps already dead from the smoke at that time. Later they took her small charred body from the ruins.

The next week I went to see Amelia. She and her smaller sister had been brought down the road to the home of an aunt who was not well herself and really not prepared to take care of them. Amelia was still almost in a state of shock. Her arms were bandaged. Her grandmother, the only mother she had really ever known, was in the hospital, badly burned.

"I looked for you," Amelia said (meaning at the time of the wake), "and you didn't come." I thought my heart would break. When she had needed me the most, I was not there. I explained to her that I had been out of town at a meeting and did not know what had happened until I returned.

"It's all right," she tried to smile. "The white girls in my class came and sat with me that night."

The lessons of learning to live together in peace are hard-learned. The experiences often are bitter and sad. There are happy ones, too. Progress sometimes seems so very, very slow that often I have thought those who expect a millennium the day after tomorrow may be disappointed. But the winds *are* changing.

Two years ago Sam, the rebellious student about whom I have told you, returned home for a visit from the Navy. Since leaving high school, he had been aboard an aircraft carrier in the Pacific, and now is helping in Vietnam. His ship had docked and set out from many ports. He had grown much taller. He was neat and clean-shaven.

"How are you getting along with the Negro problem?" he asked me, as so many of the older students do.

I told him how things had improved—how different everything is now. He seemed glad. He said he regretted that he had been such a problem in school both to himself and to others. He said that since he understood things more clearly he wished he could go back and behave differently.

"Whatever got into me?" he said. "I wasted so much time with hate."

That moment I knew that "my Sam" could have gone to

school all his life and not learned a lesson more important. I would not worry about him any more. Sam was now free of mental slavery. His children would not be shackled as he had been. In a sense, I was freer also. And this kind of experience is taking place every day now. The children are looking above and beyond us all. And they're judging us, too.

This year a white youngster who is a brilliant scholar said, in referring to the ease with which the elementary schools of the county had been desegregated from the first grade up: "I know they had to admit the Negro children because they can't run the schools without the federal money [he was referring to the Civil Rights Act, which bars financial aid to segregated schools], but I wish they could have let the Negro children come on into the schools without the threat of money." Such young people are coming face to face with tomorrow.

And just as the white student is changing his basic attitudes, so the Negro student who succeeds in this new approach to living begins to look out upon his world from a different window. All the while in this new environment, perhaps without even realizing it, he has been absorbing new things. He has seen the rewards of initiative and learning. Gradually, these and many other things have become an indispensable part of his life. He begins to see that there is a better way to live and that he can attain it. He, too, begins to look inward for solutions.

One of the Negro boys who was graduated wrote this letter:

. . . It has now been three years since my graduation. I can truly say that was a day I will never forget. It was a great honor. These opportunities come only once in a lifetime.

I'm grateful to my parents and teachers who urged me to go on. I would not give a million dollars for that experience, nor would I take a million to go through it again . . .

I learned more there in the three years than the nine years in the Negro schools. Maybe you don't know how many friends I made—how much prestige and social status I feel.

Looking back, I'm beginning to feel you can hardly blame one race because both sides have people who are mean. I don't worry now about people not recognizing me. I want to strive so that I can be worth recognizing.

6

Closing the Gaps

OUR experiences at Clinton and elsewhere in the South make it obvious that there is more involved in the education of the Negro children of the South than merely opening the doors of the white schools. In fact, to admit them into the comprehensive, college-oriented white schools, and expect the same performance of them when they have spent eight or more years (the most formative years) in an inferior segregated school, as no doubt is happening all over the South, can be cruel. With such a background, how can we assume they are "even" at the start? I do not mean "even" in the sense that we expect children to be the same, for we recognize vast differences in all children—but "even" in the sense that they have sufficient academic background in basic skills (reading, writing, arithmetic) to succeed in a public school.

You don't have to work with Negro children very long before you cease to wonder why they do not achieve more in their studies. You only marvel that they have come as far as they have, and that they are even in school. And if you are honest with yourself, you probably will have to admit that you might not have done as well in the circumstances.

Let me tell you what happened to Roberta, the Negro girl I mentioned earlier, who was so eager to come to high school. The great day came at last. Roberta kept her promise. She came to the white school. I have rarely seen such enthusiasm in a student. There she stood that hot August day in her skirt made of feed sacks, and a dingy white blouse. Her curly hair was tousled and looked as if it had not been combed for days. The black-rimmed glasses provided by public assistance kept slipping down on her nose. Her eyesight had been so neglected that she couldn't read without them. But the refreshing quality about Roberta was that material things didn't seem to matter—not yet anyway. She was as happy to be among us as if she had waited her whole life for this moment. I truly believe she had. There was something about her enthusiasm for school that seemed to come from deep inside her. I thought of Hardy's *Jude the Obscure*. "It is a city of light," Jude said when he viewed the great university from afar. "The tree of knowledge grows there. It is a place that teachers of men spring from and go to. It is what you may call a castle manned by scholarship and religion. It would just suit me."

I believed Roberta was ready to tackle her "city of light" single-handed. Her score in the mental ability tests was among the highest ever made by any student in our school. Now that she had access to a large library, she was seldom seen without an armload of books. There were few who noticed her insatiable desire for knowledge, or knew how far back into her childhood that desire went, or what security she found in the printed pages—or perhaps even cared. Roberta's faith in her own potential was deep. It was that beautiful, indomitable faith of youth. She seemed to feel that one could move mountains by sheer determination and will. When I talked to her, I felt as if I were talking to a matriarch "born before her time." There was something almost frightening about it.

Roberta was a strong girl and she would laugh heartily. She was always in a hurry, as if she had some mission to perform, or so far to go before the darkness fell. She would rush in to my office with an armload of books, never setting them down for one moment while she trailed off with her excited plans. She had everything outlined perfectly and did not allow for any setbacks. Then she would rush away, and out the school door, and up the hill to her cabin. Each day, before the sun set, she would do the work of another woman—a much older woman who had seen hard times and breadless days. When the little ones were bedded down, she would return to her borrowed books. She had to finish them on time. There was no money to pay the library fines.

I knew this child needed special attention. I would talk to her teachers. I would explain to them about her background and tell them of her tremendous desire for knowledge. I would plead for their help and compassion. I felt that if we could get her educated and into a good job, she could break the cycle of ignorance and poverty which had enslaved her family. I even thought that one day we might be able to send her to college or to a good business school.

When her name constantly appeared on the library's "overdue list," I was thrilled. It indicated to me that Roberta still loved her books. But others didn't see it this way. Her teachers said she could hold a class spellbound in telling a story, but "her written expression was poor," and this brought her grade down. They found so much wrong and so little right—and in such a short time. Roberta now began to realize her inadequacies. In the Negro elementary school she had been the top student with little effort. Now she found she had to work very hard to keep even an average grade among white students. But in spite of the handicaps, she was able to pass her courses on the knowledge she had accumulated up to now on her own, although her grades were much lower than she had been accustomed to. By the end of the year, things were beginning to happen to her, inside, which I don't suppose we will ever really understand.

In the second year the change became quite noticeable. She was more restless. Responsibilities at home began to crowd in upon her. The courses were difficult now and demanded more concentration and study. She was torn between her great desire to stay in school and succeed and her obligations to her family. Everything became complicated. By the end of the year she began to talk of finishing high school in three years, as if she knew her days in school were numbered and she would crowd as much into a short time as she possibly could. This would take summer school. And summer school costs money—a lot of money to poor people. Her mother couldn't afford it, nor did Roberta expect her to.

She never begged for help. She just announced her decisions. "I've got it all figured out," she rushed by to tell me one day at the close of school. "Mother says she can manage when the new baby comes this summer, and I've got a job helping a woman, so now I can get the $25 and go to summer school."

Too soon, I feared now, she would collide with the world outside her books where there was no opportunity, no job, nothing. She wasn't going to be ready. I advised her how we would help her seek opportunities if she would only hold on and prepare herself more thoroughly. But I wasn't sure now that she was going to give us time to help her learn how to use her talents. Already there were complaints that she was falling behind in her assignments, and other things.

We provided the money for summer school. But she began to be absent from classes now—and not always because she was needed at home. Her attitudes changed. She was more aggressive, and even at times deceitful. In the fall I asked the Negro children why Roberta was not back in school. "Don't you know," they said, "Roberta's gone and quit school?"

I found her on the street. "Why, Roberta, why?" I asked. She summed it in one sentence: "I woke up one morning and I looked about me; and I just decided it was too much to overcome."

The whole sorry scheme of things had converged upon us, and her too. We just didn't know enough to help her as she should have been helped. Roberta had come and seen for herself, and turned back. And when she turned back, a part of me went back with her.

As I continued to work with Negro students like Roberta, and watched them reach out for their "city of light" as for a brief moment she had reached out, I began to realize more than ever that there must be many such boys and girls all over the South struggling in much the same way to make something of themselves, and against the same obstacles both at home and in the school. I found myself crying out against the complacency of those who could help them in their struggle. And at the same time I came to realize how much there is to be done, how little time we have, and how little we really know about working with these children.

The teachers were right. Roberta was weak, according to the standards set for white children. She was ill-prepared for the new school. She was weak not because she lacked ability or ambition but because she had so much to battle over which she had no control. How could she have been otherwise?

Everyone knew what Roberta's failure meant to me. The Principal tried to console me. "You're an idealist," he said. And I suppose he was right. Oh, I knew Roberta was careless with her punctuation marks; that she had never had "modern math" as the white children had; that she had never written a précis; that she made errors in spoken English. But these seemed such small things compared to the potential and the spirit of the child. An older supervisor said, "You may work with fifty children and fail forty-nine times. But one day one will come through; and that will make everything worthwhile." This *was* something to look forward to; but no, the happiness and the fulfillment of human beings, and especially children, should not depend on such odds. In China or India perhaps it might be inevitable, but not in America.

There is little doubt that the average Negro child comes to us with a weak academic background. Conditions in Negro elementary schools in the rural South could have produced little else. Many of these schools, especially in the rural and mountain areas and even in some cities of the South, are very much as they might have been a quarter of a century ago. There are some Negro rural schools where the children still sit on benches made of planed boards. Often the school buses, the books, and other equipment are what the Negroes call "hand-me-downs" from the white schools. In many places the Negro teachers have none of the instructional supervision or educational materials and supplies provided ordinarily by boards of education. Whatever the teachers or the Negro parents cannot provide, the children do without. Many of these schools have no libraries at all.

I remember visiting one such school. There was only one classroom, and a small storage room perhaps six or eight feet off the main room. On one side of the storage room, shelves were nailed to the wall. This was considered "the library." The only books on those shelves were discarded ones which white people had donated. The only set of encyclopedias for the use of forty or more children was one published in the early 1900's—so outdated that they might have been just as well off without any.

In every rural Negro school I have visited, the pupil-teacher ratio has been higher than in the white schools of the same district. The teachers are overworked and much of their time is consumed with duties other than instruction. I've seen them build the fires in the big pot-bellied stove and gather the children around it so they could keep warm. Or themselves prepare lunch, so the children would have something to eat. Or divide the lunches, so that every child would have some food. Many of these teachers are their own janitors, school nurses, recreation, music, and art directors while trying to teach three to eight grades at one time.

The background of the average Negro teacher, especially in the rural South, has been a deprived background. Born in poverty, most Negro teachers are the product of the same type of schools in which they now teach. "In addition," a Negro professor told me recently, "Negro teachers on the whole have not had the supplementary opportunities of white teachers. Up until the last few years, their salaries have been relatively lower than those of white teachers; and they have not been able to provide themselves with the cultural experiences broadening to a teacher." But the teachers have done the best they could; to my mind, enough could never be said for the Negro teachers of the South. They have given children hope when there was no hope. They have kept a foot in the gates of learning until the rest of us could see the need to swing those gates open wide.

The more I worked with Negro children and realized this background, the more I began to wonder: How could we help them to improve themselves? What could be done to get these children on an equal footing with other children with whom they now must compete? Do we just turn our heads and say, "You asked for this. Make out the best you can. We've done our part by letting you come here"?

Frances, the Negro teacher, had said that day I visited her, "You have always found a few among us outstanding, but what you have missed is in not taking the potential of all of us." The big question now seems to be how to get the potential of all.

I began to read and study everythng I could find, in an attempt to discover ways to help the Negro children with whom I worked. My difficulty was that there was little information available at that time on how to work with children from minority groups and deprived backgrounds. Our faculty as a group had never discussed the education of the Negro child. We had never had one day, or even one hour, of in-service training in racial relations. I found few people, even teachers, who were willing to sit and discuss the problems of Negro children.

Because of my expressed interest in the problems of the Negro children of the South, many people and groups outside my own community did offer to help me. The American Personnel and Guidance Association, the Southern Regional Council, the Children's Bureau of the Department of Health, Education, and Welfare, and many other groups invited me to their professional meetings, where they shared their information regarding the needs of children. They sent books, pamphlets, data on research. They made it possible for me to hear American government officials, university professors, and citizens share their knowledge and experiences over the years in an attempt to improve the education and opportunities of the children of low-income and disadvantaged families. I learned many things from them and discovered ways to make opportunities available for children with whom I worked.

But most of all, as I heard them discuss the problems of the children of the nation, North and South, urban and rural; as I heard them explain how important it is that we work hard in our communities, else the nation might be in deep trouble, my faith was renewed that many citizens are deeply concerned and are working to help. I could return to my work with new hope and the knowledge that it is not wrong to care, but right and necessary. And I realized with renewed intensity that the development of the Negro children of the South for useful and productive citizenship is not only a major responsibility in which we each have a part. It is a "new frontier" in education.

There are, to my mind, very practical reasons for concern about the education of the Negro children of the

South. Since the federal government (by the Civil Rights Act of 1964) now requires desegregation, or a "pledge" of plans for desegregation, before releasing funds to school systems, the process of desegregation will take on an unprecedented impetus in the next few years. The schools of the South cannot be operated adequately without federal funds. This means that whereas at present about fifteen percent of the 3.5 million Negro children of the seventeen Southern and border states are now attending school with whites (six percent in the South proper), it is very probable that within the next five years, not the token six percent or the over-all fifteen percent but the vast majority of Negro children will be in predominantly white schools. The question arises: how will the quality of the education in Southern schools be affected by the entrance of so many Negro children who are recognized generally as being inadequately prepared?

My own experiences have been with a small group of Negro children who never at any time comprised more than three percent of the student body, and who were in such a minority that their presence did not affect the total school program one way or another. Yet through them I could see that in the very Deep South where the Negroes in many communities make up fifty to seventy-five percent of the population, the children are so poorly prepared for modern schools that without very special programs the academic standards of the entire school system would have to be lowered if they were to realize any measure of success. This is one of the great problems which plague white parents, and understandably so where the schools will consist of a majority of children from extremely deprived backgrounds. A weak or "watered-down" school program would not solve the Negro child's problems, because even though he might "succeed" in such a program it would not prove adequate to the demands being made upon him in today's world. This would never do, nor would I ever suggest such. And without intensive preparation and very special help, the talent I see among the Negro children is literally "going down the drain" for lack of nurture and concern. Thus, programs of the highest standards of excellence are necessary not only to safeguard the proper development of the Negro children, but for the well-being of all of our children.

Furthermore, the Negro students in today's desegregated classrooms are now in the process of becoming what they will be tomorrow. The Negro leaders of tomorrow are sitting in those classrooms also. What happens to these children today will in large measure determine the quality of their citizenship and their leadership in the future. So often I have thought how carefully we would teach them today *if we were wise*. For if we do not, they will educate themselves in their own way. They will attach values to whatever symbols in their environment they desire. "Attaching symbols" is much easier in our day than even a few years ago, because of the vast news and information media and the close proximity with which people live and spread ideas.

For these two practical reasons, aside from the humanitarian reasons, poor planning now for these children is dangerous to the nation. As in the case of Roberta, I am concerned how these children will use their gifted minds in later years. Will Roberta seek outlets for her brilliant mind in some hate group? Well she might, for life hit her very hard. Or, in some way, will we be able to take up again and educate her so that she can use her talents for the betterment of herself and her fellow man?

All of this, then, can be boiled down to one thing: there is an immediate need for far-reaching educational programs for these children, and they must be provided in today's schools. We are in need of programs of excellence and high standards so bold that, to my mind, the entire educational system of the South needs to be overhauled. I would even go further and say that this is one of the moral imperatives of our time. Until desegregation in the South is completed from the first grade up, and especially for those children coming into our schools today in the upper grades, we must provide programs of cultural and educational enrichment for them—extra things to make up for whatever they have been denied or need to compete with other children— if we are to educate today's Negro children as they should be educated.

The idea of compensatory education for the Negro in America is not a new idea, but it has never been tried on a national scale as can be done with our present resources. Although it will perhaps take a generation to realize any large-scale results, it is still the most humanitarian, and the most economical, way out of our dilemma.

Alice Lee Humphrey, a retired North Carolina teacher, has told the story of a first-grade child who was asked to start counting at "29" and continue to "100." The child began to stroke her red gingham dress and labored desperately, muttering numbers to herself: 1, 2, 3 . . . The teacher prodded her sharply, telling her that she must begin instantly at "29" as she had been instructed. The child replied, "Tarnation! I got to get thar' fust."

Miss Humphrey's student spoke for all children who are

behind in their school work. They have got to "get there first." And we have got to provide programs in the schools which take up wherever these children are when they come to us, and progress from that point. It means very simply that if a child is fourteen years old and in the ninth grade and he still reads on a sixth-grade level, and he is capable of learning (as practically all children really are), then we must provide special help and instruction for him. It is not likely that he will do very well in his classes otherwise.

This may sound simple. But it is one of the most difficult problems facing schools today. Such help calls for special classes, individual work with students, money to provide special services, and a hundred other things—but very possible things in America today. With the help of the vast resources of the federal government, we now can furnish special opportunities to deprived school children as never before. Under the National Defense Education Act, the Economic Opportunity Act, and other recent legislation; and by locally providing small amounts of money to match federal funds, we can equip our school libraries and our science laboratories, we can train teachers, provide jobs for children in need, and do many other things which will benefit not only the Negro children but all children. The success of these programs will depend upon the desires of the communities, for the overriding requirement in most of the new federal legislation to aid education is that the local communities must decide for themselves what needs to be done. It is now a question of whether we care enough to look about us, plan what should be done, and set ourselves to the task of doing it.

"Improvement programs," providing compensatory opportunities for disadvantaged children, are already fairly widespread in the great metropolitan areas of the North, East, and West. These programs have taken on various names in cities where they have been started with or without federal aid and grants. Perhaps the most far-reaching of these programs has been the "Higher Horizons Program" started in New York City in 1956. This was one of the first large-scale, systematic programs designed to meet the educational needs of disadvantaged children.

Jacob Landers, coordinator of the program, described the children admitted to this program (Negroes, Puerto Ricans, whites) as children who "collectively suffered from all the ills which a modern society can visit upon the children unfortunate enough to live in its city slums." Many came from families on public welfare; many came from broken homes. And many of them were "latchkey children, wearing around their necks the key which was mute evidence of an empty apartment when they returned from school."

The results of this program have been astounding, and beyond anything we would ever have dreamed possible twenty years ago. With the special help and attention provided, the verbal IQ's of these children were raised, their reading ability was increased, and the number of drop-outs was reduced drastically. The number of these children who went on to college was enormous compared to what it had been before. They were accepted in some of the great universities of the nation and were able to perform success-fully—and all because they were given special attention, not prematurely but before it was too late.

In view of what we know about the education of cultur-ally deprived children, vast numbers of them could benefit enormously from preschool training. For the disadvantaged child, the poor child, the neglected child—whatever you want to call him—the earlier in his life that special opportunities are provided, the greater is his chance of success.

The need for preschool training was brought home to me last year when I spent an afternoon in a first-grade classroom in a mountain school nearby. Although this is a segregated white school because no Negroes live within a radius of many miles, the children are so lacking in opportunities that they would be comparable to typical Negro children the same age in the rural South. This mountain school is in an extremely depressed area which was once a prosperous mining community. The mines are now closed, but the people stay on. The fathers of many of the two hundred children who attend school here had been killed in the mines; and most of the families are on public assistance.

I accompanied an elementary-school supervisor who is a master teacher and reading specialist. Her purpose that day was to work with the new teacher who had just come to her job and decide what needed to be done for the children, as they were so disorganized. It was now January, and although these children had been in school since September, a great many of them had not even started to read. When we arrived, the new teacher had the children lined up and she was showing them how to wash their hands and use soap.

One little fellow slept with his head on the desk practically the entire time we were there. The teacher said, "I believe there is something wrong with that child, but I haven't had time to get to him. He sleeps all the time."

There was a little girl with long, straggling, blond hair, a calico dress that came almost to her ankles, and old-fashioned high-topped shoes that no doubt were handed

down from an older brother or sister. At every opportunity this child would grab the big broom from the corner
and start sweeping the room. The teacher said this was the
only thing in school she liked to do. I must admit I have
never seen such a thorough job of sweeping. Although the
broom was very heavy for her to handle, she managed to
get it into every nook and corner. She even moved the
desks and swept under them. When she got to the little boy
who was asleep, she gave his desk a firm kick and swept
under it, and then very gently she tugged him back into
place. He only roused himself long enough to turn his head
from one side to the other. "This is what Mother does at
home," she said proudly. This child was not ready to read
or write or use crayons and other tools as might be expected of most six-and-a-half-year-olds. Some of the children cried constantly. When asked if they liked school,
they were frank to say, "No," that they wanted to go
home.

The master teacher took the children in groups of three
and four to small tables. She put her arms around them. She
told them stories. She asked them questions. I watched their
eyes light up. They began to smile. In fifteen minutes she
was able to elicit enthusiastic responses from them; she
knew how to reach small children. When we left, they
were begging her to tell them more stories. And we would
not have left when we did, except that the buses had come
to take the children home. But when we came away, the
master teacher was very distressed. "They are not ready
for school," she said. "They are not ready."

Most of these children will not be ready for the second
grade. And by the time these children reach the third or
fourth grade they will be very far behind, and it will be

difficult for them ever to catch up. In other words, as someone has said: "The longer they stay in school, the dumber they seem to get." They will regress rather than progress. In fact, many of these disadvantaged children who are perfectly normal children in the first grades will decline in their performance each year so that by the time they are in the ninth grade, if they are still in school (and a large percent will not be), they are considered retarded.

It is a well-established fact now that children who have had kindergarten experience are more nearly ready for school. This is not to say that every child should go to kindergarten, but those who come from homes which are extremely deprived do need special help in getting ready for school. In the special preschool programs, the teachers read to them, tell them stories, create interest in school. The children begin to learn how to work and play with other children, how to take care of themselves away from home, how to go through the lunch line, how to begin to relate with adults outside the home, and many other things which make them more secure in a group. The teachers can also begin to work with the parents, and see that the children have medical examinations so that physical defects are identified early. The "Head Start" or preschool programs now possible through federal aid will do much to alleviate these conditions and prepare children for school.

Some people have the idea that preschool training will automatically solve the problems of culturally deprived children. Certainly it will not. Preschool training is only the first step—the first of many steps which must be taken to help the disadvantaged child. My experiences indicate that these children are going to need help all through school and even into college and higher training.

We must look in a different way at those Negro children who are now in the desegregated schools and have not had preschool training, as practically none has. It would be callous to give them up as a bad job. They are not responsible for the retarded academic state in which they find themselves. As one Negro girl put it: "It is your teen-age group which is having the trouble now and will be the most trouble to you. We were not prepared for the desegregated schools. But it will be different for the ones coming on if we start now—and don't wait any longer to get them the help they need."

These children, who tend to have such a poor estimate of themselves and their possibilities, must realize some measure of success. Their entire achievement in school hinges on this. How many children, and especially Negro children, have I heard say, "There's no need for me to stay in school. I can't pass." I am convinced that they have given up because performance has been expected of them for which they are not ready. They have met failure at every turn, until leaving school actually becomes the most sensible solution, for no individual keeps on at something if he is constantly pronounced a failure. Common logic tells him to begin to seek alternatives in areas where he can succeed.

Perhaps the most important part of the instructional program is the provision for special help in reading. Unless a child is able to read and comprehend what he has read, he will have difficulty in most of his subjects. We are finding that as many as one third of the white children and a still larger percent of the Negro children coming into high school are not able to read with competence. Yet, in spite of the fact that everyone recognizes the great need for improvement in reading skill, it is rare indeed that special reading instruction is provided in the upper grades; and the majority of high-school English teachers really are not trained to teach reading, nor do they have the time.

Through remedial classes, summer programs, and the like, these children can receive special instruction in phonics, vocabulary, word recognition, comprehension, and reading speed. Where special programs are in operation, the teachers report that students begin to read more on their own and for pleasure. They can be encouraged to build their own home libraries even with paperback books. Every child should have his own bookshelf. I know a few Negro children who are doing just that because they have become interested in reading; and it seems to increase their appreciation of good books.

Older Negro children in school today are becoming very conscious of the value of reading. Some seem to have an almost insatiable desire to own books. One boy I know frequents sales and bargain basements. He buys discarded books—sometimes for a nickel or a dime. The titles or print don't seem to make a great deal of difference. He just wants to own his own books. Of late I have noticed Negro students and their parents in bookstores, something I never saw in this part of the South five years ago. One day I received a large box of paperback books from a New York book reviewer who thought the Negro children might use them or they could be placed in the library. They were mostly classics. I never got the books to the library because the day I opened the box I asked every Negro child who happened by my office if he would like to look through the books and take whatever he wanted home with him. Some went out with their arms full.

And while we are helping the Negro children improve

their reading and develop an appreciation for good books, they need help with their speech. They are accustomed to the dialect of the Negro of the South, which is a handicap to them in the modern school. They use such words as "axt" for "ask," "dunna" for "dinner," and so on. Many Negro teachers have perpetuated this dialect in instructing them. The white children notice the old-fashioned words and expressions, whereas the Negro children do not because they have never heard anything else. Although I have always lived in the South, I often have difficulty understanding Negro children and have to ask them to repeat words or explain what they mean by certain expressions. These children also need concentrated help in writing. Apparently the manner in which they are accustomed to speaking has much to do with their writing, for they often write words as they sound in dialect.

In addition to receiving special help in basic subjects, I feel that Negro children should be exposed to at least one activity of a cultural nature such as music, art, or drama. For the average Negro child, this part of his education has been sadly neglected.

We notice a great change in Negro children when they begin to participate in group activities and explore cultural subjects. In fact, we find that numbers of them have considerable talent in music and art, as well as a capacity for the study of foreign languages. Some teachers say that Negro children grasp languages quickly because they have been taught by rote—that is, by listening and memorizing—and that they are adept at mimicking. I do not know whether there is anything to this or not. I do know that in our school many Negro children show an unusual interest in foreign languages.

There is another reason why Negro children should be encouraged to explore cultural activities. Today's Negro children are the product of a restless age, and like all of us, they are going to need to know how to find peace of mind in the midst of the uncertainties and the turmoil about us. The arts provide outlets, escapes, and balances for people, and enrich their lives as well.

And in my own "higher horizons," I would provide for the Negro children extra experiences of every kind possible and practical. These would start at home. We don't have to have federal grants to take these children to the art museums, the free concerts, the courthouse, the public libraries; or to the banks and the factories. Many Negro children have never been to any of these right in their own towns. During these trips, time should be provided for the children to talk with officials, doctors, businessmen, and people of importance in the community. If they can hear older citizens explain what a difficult time they had and how they succeeded in spite of it, how they made their way up in the world, it proves to them that obstacles can be overcome. I have found that the truly great people are always willing to give of themselves. Somehow, as busy as they are, they are never too busy to talk with young people—black or white.

In our schools today we should work intensely with Negro boys to impress upon them the responsibilities of being the head of the house. In the same way, we should instill in the Negro girls pride in the arts of homemaking, the care of the home, and the proper rearing of children. In this way, the Negro family will be strengthened. The children will have examples after which they can pattern their lives.

I have often been discouraged at the number of Negro girls who seem to attach some stigma to taking home-economics classes in high school. I believe they associate classes in sewing, cooking, child development, and the like, with domestic service; and we know they are trying to get away from this. But they do need such classes, not only to improve their own persons, but to help improve the Negro home and their family life. Home-economics teachers can be of inestimable value to Negro girls. They can help them with personal grooming, cleanliness, moral values and in many ways other teachers cannot.

I have mentioned how the Negro child seems to feel he has no heritage or social status; one of our major responsibilities in his education would seem to be to help instill in him a sense of pride in his race. Here there is much that we can do.

We must encourage the Negro child to preserve his own unique heritage which has contributed vastly to the culture of the South. We can remind him of great Negro leaders who served and are serving America with distinction. We must be sure that he does not feel ashamed of being a Negro. For as we move further into integration, there is danger that this very thing may happen if we do not show him another road.

There are many ways to instill racial pride. Sometimes I have thought that the Negro schools and Negro organizations are doing more along these lines than we are. In the more progressive segregated Negro schools today, great emphasis is being placed on the development of racial pride. The children are encouraged to read the biographies of great Negroes. They have plays enacting moments in history in which Negroes have had a part. And there are special days called "Heritage Days."

The National Urban League, which has done so much to secure equal opportunities for Negro citizens, recently published a brochure containing pictures of outstanding present-day Negroes who have achieved success in various fields. The purpose of this brochure is to help provide motivation and incentive for Negro youngsters. The idea is that if they can see someone of their own race and nearer their own age who has achieved success, they will be encouraged to go on themselves.

Negro children are proud when one refers to the accomplishments of their people. I saw this clearly the day of the march on Washington. Many Negro students seemed to "drift by" my office that day. I think they may have anticipated trouble, and they seemed relieved that all went well. William was among the first to come. I never saw him so happy before.

"Well, how do you feel today?" I asked him.

"We're coming," he said with a big smile. "Slowly but surely we're coming."

And another boy who was with him added, "I'm so proud of my people today."

In the education of Negro children today there is a great need for strong guidance programs in the elementary as well as in the high schools. Through guidance programs, the children have the advantages of services they might not otherwise get. And, of course, the heart of any guidance program is the provision for counseling, where the child has access to one special person always available to help him—someone who sees no problem too small to discuss, and no "problem child," only a "child with problems."

I feel that during these times there is a great need for "incentive counseling" and for plain, simple "encouragement." Through such counseling, which need not be the prerogative of professionals but can come from parents, teachers, neighbors—all who touch the lives of these children—we can help them to raise their own estimate of themselves. This means that you let the child know you care what happens to him and that you have faith in him just as he is. I have noticed that teachers who encourage their students are able to see accomplishments in them we never dreamed were possible. I have seen struggling Negro students take the hardest courses and succeed mainly because they felt encouragement from the teacher.

There is an imperative need for teachers who are trained in intercultural relations and work with culturally deprived children. We need not only teachers who are able to relate instruction to the needs of individual children, but teachers who are aware, just plain old-fashioned "aware," that circumstances can affect children. From what I have seen, I would say that in far too many places this insight is sadly lacking.

For example, at one Southern conference I attended, I heard public-school teachers ask: "What would you do if you could not look at a Negro child in your class?" "How would you teach the Civil War now that there are Negro children in the class?" I don't know how they had been "teaching the Civil War," but they seemed to be completely thrown off base now that there were Negro children in the class. And another: "Why are we so concerned with the desires and welfare of a minority?" I have known teachers to consult school authorities on whether they should show an educational film in their classrooms if the film had a Negro in it.

These seemingly ridiculous situations become very real problems to many teachers. They indicate that many of those who are now largely responsible for the education of the Negro children of the South have, in reality, not yet desegregated themselves. But I am not so concerned about those who question, for they are in the process of finding answers; my concern is for those who do not yet recognize their prejudices and are innocently inflicting them on young minds.

The children know exactly which teachers are fairly free of prejudices and which are not. This comes to light when a Negro child says, "I would rather not be in that class—I can't explain it—it's just the way the teacher looks at me." A Negro girl confides: "We can tell when the teachers are prejudiced. They are the ones who always seem to be worried about saying the wrong thing in front of us— always trying hard not to. You can tell when it comes natural. There is a tense feeling when you talk with them. It is like they are afraid to be seen talking to you. It is that something that is between us. You can feel it."

There is much talk now of the kinds of teachers and other workers who are most successful in helping disadvantaged children. This is one of the most important things we need to know in carrying out the anti-poverty programs, because everything depends upon the type of people who are placed in charge of these children and of the programs for them and their parents. When we are able to identify those qualities in human beings that make them more effective in motivating children to bring out the best that is in them, we will have come a long way. I would not attempt to say I have the answers, but I can tell you, out of my own experiences in working with Negro and white children in the mountains some of the characteristics of those teachers who seem to be most successful.

First, they are people who have faith in humanity. They respect each individual as a human being in his own right. They do not think so rigidly that they try to force the children into their patterns. They are not shocked by the children. They understand them and respond to their critical needs. They are much less self-centered than most people and they place the well-being of the child above everything else. They enjoy helping people and seeing them succeed.

It has often been said that frequently the people who are most successful in working with underprivileged children come from deprived backgrounds themselves and are thus able to understand the problems of these children to a greater extent. In many cases I have seen that this is true. Many teachers who have struggled for an education or who have had some difficulty and solved it are able to understand problems that others might not, because they have experienced the problems themselves. On the other hand, I have seen these very people, whom one would expect to have the most understanding because they themselves have endured almost identical problems, turn out, for some strange reason, to be the least patient with the children who need them. Theirs is a "nobody helped *me* and look what I did" attitude. Somehow they seem to feel that they have conquered their problem, or overcome the same type of background, and they cannot understand why these children cannot do the same. Then, many, I think, actually do not want to be reminded of hard times after they come out of them. They identify themselves with the "gifted," never thinking for one moment that in this "ragamuffin" child there may be gifts undreamed of.

I have worked with many teachers who are the product of very sheltered lives where they have had every opportunity; and they seem to have the most compassion. So much depends upon the individual, his outlook on his own life and on other lives about him. These people who have had more advantages seem to be able to accept children wherever they are and whatever they are. I think it might be because they have accepted themselves. Most of all, and of this much I am very sure—they are people who care what happens to children.

Whatever qualities the teacher may or may not possess, we know that his personality is a major factor in the success of these children. It is most essential that a teacher in charge of deprived children should maintain a "creative atmosphere" in the classroom. At this point, we do not know exactly what these children can do or what their potential is because they have never been given an opportunity for any of these things to come out into the open. If the teacher sets his standards so high that they become impossible, or if he superimposes his ways upon the children and makes them feel failure unless they do things exactly "his way," we may never have an opportunity to know their capabilities.

A dedicated teacher can perform miracles in working with these children. I have known many such great teachers in the Kentucky mountains. There the teachers have never known any other than deprived children.

In one of the most distressed areas in the region of the

Big Sandy River, there is an old bandmaster loved by all who have ever come under his direction. It is said that perhaps he has done more to teach a real love of music than any university in the area. This man was born and reared in the mountains. He left them only long enough to serve in the Second World War. For more than thirty years he has driven to as many as ten schools a week—over crooked and treacherous mountain roads, through hollows and across creeks. In the back of his car he carries a set of beat-up musical instruments for children who could never hope to own their own. He uses the same instruments for ten schools. From his classes have come some of the great musicians and teachers of the area. Once, after some university professors had come to the mountains to judge his students in a music contest, one of them said, "When I saw this man and what he had to work with and what he had produced, it brought tears to my eyes; and I came away in humility."

In our efforts to "close the gap" we also desperately need to draw Negro parents closer to the school. Few will come on their own. This means that we must go to them. The parents must know that they are wanted and needed for the sake of their children. I have never seen a Negro parent refuse to come to the school who was asked to come. Nor have I seen one refuse to help in some way when he was asked to help in a way that he could. Sometimes, if the Negro parent is given the smallest responsibility toward a meeting or a program, a whole new world of communication opens. One Negro mother I know was asked to provide cookies for a class party. She was as proud as if she had been asked to make the cakes for an exclusive affair—

which, of course, she had done many times for white people, but never for the school. Most of all, it made her child proud of her and showed them both that she was needed and appreciated. Negro parents today are ready to help. They know education is the avenue to an escape from poverty. Will we use their readiness to help? Will we make them feel welcome and wanted?

Since many people contribute in one way or another to the education of the Negro child, there is need to identify and use those people in every community who seem to be most talented in working with the underprivileged. Every community has them. They may be poor; they may be uneducated; they may not even be able to read or write. Yet they have ways of reaching troubled families and they have been doing so for many, many years, and long before we ever heard of an "anti-poverty" program. I have found that one of the best ways to locate these "natural Samaritans" is to notice those to whom the Negro children or their parents turn in time of real trouble. Sometimes it will be the groceryman at the corner store, the family doctor, the Sunday School teacher, or some such person who through the years has won a place in their hearts by his understanding and proven friendship.

I mention this type of person because I have worked with such people who have helped me with Negro children and other children when many have failed, and I know their influence. For example, there is "on the hill" an old Negro grandmother who is highly respected by her neighbors and their children. Because she has been thrifty all her life, she is just a little better off than most of the other Negroes in her neighborhood. She owns a refrigerator and a sewing machine, and she has screens on her windows. In her quiet way she is able to go into the homes and find out exactly why the children are not in school. She goes because she believes that children should be in school. She is more successful than most attendance officers because the Negro families confide in her. Her life has been an example for them. She is one of them, and they look up to her.

Then there is an elderly Negro man who is highly respected by both races. For years now he has kept a Scout troop in existence with little help from the outside. Today this troop has grown to such numbers that it is almost too much for one person—especially one of his age. This man has taken young Negro boys who otherwise would have "gone to the streets," and worked with them and instilled in them a desire to stay in school and become useful citizens. He has also instilled in them the desire to help the younger children. Today when I talk with Negro boys they tell me how they plan to keep this troop going. Without realizing it, this man has trained future leaders.

Of course, the most important of all the "higher horizons" is the one I would call "the horizon of the heart." Here we enter the realm of true understanding. We become involved in the lives of these boys and girls as we would in the lives of our own. Such understanding will never be legislated, nor can money buy it. It must come from the heart and from the conscience.

If these Negro children can come through the first year in the desegregated high school, and better still, through the second year, their chances of finishing high school are very, very good. The big drop-out occurs between the eighth and ninth grades. This seems to be a crucial point.

Many youngsters are afraid to make the change to the new school and somehow never get there.

Many who experience failure in the ninth grade either withdraw then or become discouraged. They may return the second year to try again. If they experience success, they usually stay. On the other hand, if they come back and again are "pushed aside," they usually withdraw before midterm. By this time many are old enough not to be included in the compulsory-school laws and, more often than not, they never return to school.

The children who do come through high school appear to emerge much stronger in every way. They are not only stronger in their studies, but they seem to have learned to cope with the world about them. They are more tolerant, and white students are more tolerant of them. By this time they have begun to feel that they are a part of the school and often they come back for visits. They have made friends. They have proven themselves. They feel more equal.

One Negro girl who dropped out of school twice, and is now a senior, summed it up. "The problems don't seem so big as they once did," she said.

And truly they are not. These children are now ready to face crucial decisions—that is, enter college or some other form of higher training, or the world of work. These decisions call for different types of help and present new problems for the Negro student, but also wonderful and challenging opportunities.

7

The Spirit Maketh the Master

IN the seventh year of desegregation at the Clinton High School, there were fifteen new Negro students. Among them were eight youngsters from a coal-mining area in our county, about fifteen miles from town. These children had been attending a small Negro high school about twenty-five miles away in an adjoining county. One boy in this group was in his third year of high school. He was tall, well-groomed, mannerly, and stood very much above the others in accomplishments. He came so highly recommended that he was placed in charge of the younger Negro students on the school bus.

His greatest concern that first day did not seem to be for himself but for the younger children who had been entrusted to his care. He was much like a father to them and advised them carefully. "You are not ready for algebra," he said to one. "You've got to review your arithmetic—remember what the teacher told you." I noticed that the children respected his advice. Some did not know their birth dates—that is, they knew the month and day but not the year in which they were born. Robyn very quietly furnished the information. Apparently he had memorized the dates in preparation for registration.

He waited patiently until all the children were enrolled, including his younger brother, who was a sophomore in high school and an excellent student. Then he stepped forward and presented a report card showing straight "A" grades from his former school. He requested the most advanced subjects, including higher mathematics and physics. I explained to him that there might be some adjustment in coming from a school of a hundred pupils to a school of over twelve hundred and that he might expect the courses to be more difficult. He replied, "That's what I'm asking for. I've read over a hundred books this summer and attended summer school in preparation for this."

I asked him to tell me something about himself; the Negro youngsters had come with no records from the segregated school other than a report card. He explained that in the school he had been attending there were only eight or ten pupils to a class. He recognized that his opportunities had been limited, but he said he had had a very fine mathematics teacher and this was his favorite subject. He expressed confidence in his abilities in this field, and he said he might like to prepare for work in mathematics or science. He hoped to attend college, but did not know how or where.

I learned that he was also active in his small county church, where he taught a class of boys, and that he had served as a counselor at the church camp in the summer. He tended the church grounds and built the fires for the Sunday meetings in the winter. After school, he coached the neighborhood Negro boys in basketball at the churchyard, although he had never been on a real team himself.

He explained how he had practiced ball all his life, as country boys do, without a real team or a real coach, and said he wanted to try out for the team.

"One of my greatest ambitions," he said, "has been to some day make a *real* team." He spoke with the gentility of the old Southern Negro. And like many people from remote sections of Appalachia, he used expressions which could often be traced to Elizabethan English.

In the days ahead, I would come to lean on Robyn. When problems with Negro children were difficult and discouraging, he helped me. He had ways of reaching the children—ways I could not fathom. While playing ball after school in the churchyard, he helped instill in them good attitudes toward work and school. He tutored some who were failing their classes. He was like a missionary moving about among his own people and all the while pushing on himself. I saw his brilliant mind tested both in equations and in human relations. He showed a compassion for his people I had not seen in youth before—a compassion that seemed to transcend all the petty things about us. He was leader, diplomat, scholar—always a little ahead of the other Negro students, yet never unmindful of those behind him, so that every so often he would look back to see where they were and stop and pick them up. Truly, the elements seemed so mixed in him that I thought of Shakespeare's lines: "Nature might stand up, and say to all the world, This was a man!"

But like the other Negro children who had come, Robyn lived from day to day. He only knew that he wanted to go on and make something of himself. I only knew that he must go on. We had no idea how this would become possible—just faith that in America a young man of this caliber would not be denied an opportunity. There was much to make up in the two years before high-school graduation if Robyn was to be ready for college. He had never taken a standardized test, and now he would have to go through the complicated college-entrance examinations. This lack of experience in taking tests might make a difference. Would the colleges understand? He had practically no practice in writing compositions—the basic activity in most freshmen college English courses. And no languages. But we would do the best we could and lay the groundwork carefully in preparation for the day that some great college would give him a chance.

We planned his studies as if he were going to Harvard or Yale, knowing full well that such could never be. He took extra classes, carried practice books home at night, worked to improve his vocabulary, and continued his outside reading—all of this in addition to practicing ball until late every afternoon and then walking many miles to his home. When classes were difficult and Robyn began to realize how poorly prepared he really was for the large high school, he was able to look at things philosophically and take the setbacks. He was not afraid of hard work, either physical or mental. This was greatly in our favor. He mowed lawns, served as carpenter's helper, washed windows, dug ditches. He saved every penny he could earn, taking out only enough for necessary clothes and the "special shoes" each boy had to buy who went out for basketball. No boy ever worked harder.

"I've got to make a 'good representation' of myself," he said in his quiet, determined way. "I'm concerned about preparing myself for this new age and being ready to help." And off he went, with the basketball shoes slung over his shoulder. He had been permitted to try out for the "real team." His dream had come true.

The weeks passed, and the time came for the basketball uniforms to be handed out in preparation for the first big game of the season. Sixteen boys were lined up in the school gymnasium. Fifteen uniforms were handed out. Robyn was the sixteenth boy. The white boys bowed their heads in shame.

"You had better talk with him in the morning," the principal said when the news came. Everyone knew what playing ball meant to Robyn. How could I talk with him? How could I explain something that was contrary to everything I believed in? I've never understood why any boy who wanted to play ball wouldn't be allowed to. The night was sleepless.

The next morning Robyn came as he had been asked to do. I tried to explain the situation to him as best I knew. There was no easy way. We just had to face the fact that the time had not come for a Negro to be on the ball team without disquieting effects. A neighboring team with whom we were to compete had sent word that there would be trouble if Robyn was allowed to play. There was real fear that harm might come to him if he did. It was too much of a risk. Those in authority could see the risks involved. I could only see the risk to Robyn's ambitions and dreams.

He listened to my feeble explanations. He did not say a word. I do believe, had he been less a man, he would have cried. When I explained as much as I knew to explain, he asked: "Are they going to let my brother play?"

"I do not know, Robyn. I do not know how things will be next year." He looked far off.

My job was over. It was the worst, the most unpleasant

job I have ever been called upon to perform as a teacher. God grant me strength if I ever have to go through it again. I had been used to soften the cruelest thing that can happen to a young person—the crushing of an ambition.

Robyn continued to sit and look out the window as if in a daze. And what he must have thought in those moments I don't think anybody will ever really know. I am sure he saw through all of us quite plainly. Would he now become bitter and resentful? Would he come to feel that no matter how hard he tried he didn't really have a chance? Would he give up? I had seen this happen to other children in similar circumstances.

While he sat there as if trying to make up his mind about all of us, I kept thinking: There must be another way— there's got to be another way—I could not leave him there. It was too cruel. If Robyn were my own child, and this very thing had happened to him, what would I say? Then I knew I would not be teacher, counselor, or public servant. I would take over as a "human being."

"Robyn," I tried to reason with him, "sometimes there are things that are so beyond our control that trying to reach them is like batting one's head against a stone wall."

"I know," he said, "I know," in a far-off way.

"Sometimes we don't understand why things are as they are. We know they are not right. Yet we are helpless to change them." He listened carefully, but in reserve. I went on.

"And sometimes, Robyn, depending on the strength of the individual, there can be triumph in acceptance . . . Do you see a way that you could triumph in this experience and emerge a stronger person?" After a while he turned his head away from the window and looked at me directly across the desk.

We talked about how important it was that he must go on—how he must be ready when the time came—how difficult it was going to be to find a college where he would not only be accepted but could earn his way—how many things there were to do besides play ball—maybe this was a blessing—now he would have more time for his studies and the entrance examinations.

"I could use that," he said.

When he left, I knew that Robyn had come to the first great crossroad in his life. I was not sure which direction he would take. Could he find triumph in acceptance? Could he find a method of compensation?

I didn't hear much more from him that year, but I saw his name on the school's honor roll. Occasionally, he came by to pick up more practice books or college catalogues. An older teacher remarked one day, "That boy has the most brilliant mind of any student I have ever taught."

In the spring of that year he came to tell me that he had definitely decided to go to college, that he must now find a college where he could be accepted and where he could work his way. He said he had saved $150 and he hoped to get another $150 from odd jobs and manual labor in the summer. He had done his part. Now I would do mine. We still had a year in which to prepare. Robyn, of course, was only one of many Negro students who would be planning for the years ahead.

In all of my work with Negro children, I have felt that helping them to plan for the future is the most challenging thing. It is a wonderful privilege to see a life seemingly destined to hopelessness turned into one of purpose and usefulness. At the same time, watching Negro children struggle to realize their ambitions in a land where there is still very much discrimination has been one of my more difficult experiences. While we cannot see an end to this discrimination, we can see the beginning of the end.

We know that many of the Negro's problems are dependent upon his economic status. It is essential then that he be able to earn a living. He will become a self-supporting citizen only when he is properly prepared for gainful employment, when he has developed skills which are in demand. In America today there are twice as many unemployed Negroes as unemployed whites. The situation is critical among eighteen- and nineteen-year olds, especially in the large cities. The Negro's unemployment problems are intensified by the fact that today's young Negroes are entering the labor market at a time when the job-swallowing effects of automation are staggering. The technological revolution which is presently taking thousands of jobs from the labor market adds to his dilemma, for he has depended on going into unskilled labor. Until recently, there has not been the slightest inkling that by the 1960's new kinds of work might be opened to Negroes, that people would be asking to employ him. He has not had the time or the opportunity to prepare for new types of work. Nor has he had the incentive to train for a lifetime of work in a field in which up to now he had no future. But the picture is changing rapidly. The question whether Negroes should prepare themselves for a variety of occupations is no longer debatable.

Our first responsibility, then, is to encourage the young Negro to complete high school if he is at all capable of doing so. Today a high-school diploma, little as it may represent to many, is the first requirement for employment. It is also a requirement for an apprenticeship in many trades and even for many training opportunities in the armed services. Only recently one of our Negro students applied for a simple, routine job of washing bottles in a laboratory. This boy had not finished high school. The personnel director liked him very much and wanted to help him, but said, "Today we rarely employ a person who does not have a high-school diploma. This is a 'must.' I just don't see how we can help him."

It is going to be extremely difficult for this young man to find gainful and permanent employment without a high-school diploma. A recent study of the Negro students who withdrew from our school before graduation and who did not go on to any other type of training revealed that the majority are unemployed. The small percent who have work are engaged only part-time or in low-paying jobs as filling-station attendants or tending lawns and gardens.

A high-school diploma is the first requirement, but it is really only the beginning. Unless the high school has strong vocational programs which prepare young people to go directly into jobs, as few in the South do, the graduating student cannot possibly have more than a basic, general education. Considering the background of the average Negro youngster coming into the newly desegregated schools today, he does well if he attains just this. It is not likely that he will be able to accomplish much without additional training of some kind, however. He still has no marketable skill.

I thought Jennie, a Negro girl who was recently graduated from high school, expressed this very well. She returned to the school one day this fall to get information on some type of additional training. She came into my office dressed neatly and in an attractive new hairdo. She had been employed temporarily during the summer and had saved all her earnings so that now she could go on. Originally she had planned to take a training course in practical nursing, but by the time she got the money to enter, the classes were closed for the year. She said, "They tell me up there on the hill that I just ought to get myself a job and go to work. I said, 'Man, what you think I'm prepared to do? I ain't got nothing to offer nobody. I got to get myself some trainin', and that's why I come back down here this morning.' " Practically every day now Negro high-school graduates come back to the high school and ask for help in finding employment. Some have been away as much as two years; they are now twenty and twenty-one years old. They tell me how they have tried to find good jobs and failed because of their lack of training.

The majority of public high schools in the South today are "college-oriented" schools. That is, the programs of instruction are geared to the needs of the upper- and middle-class youngsters who will go to college. We have given little attention to the children—more than fifty percent—who do not go to college. We desperately need more vocational and technical training in our public high schools, or in conjunction with them, for those students who do not desire to attend college or other higher training, or cannot do so, and will have to go immediately from high school into the labor market. We are making considerable progress here, but not fast enough.

The Negro boys need to learn skills which are in demand, rather than some of the skills being taught which are not in particular demand. An extreme example is the agriculture program which in most Southern schools is one of the few vocational programs available to boys, if not the only one. The number of farm workers needed is decreasing rapidly as we move from a rural to an urban society and as machinery is increasingly able to produce the same amount of food with two men that it used to take one hundred to produce manually. Yet we continue to spend millions of dollars a year on this program in the public schools, and do not provide programs in line with industry—where the most jobs are. We should be teaching these boys basic technological skills which are necessary for the jobs that exist, the jobs where there is a demand.

In view of these conditions, it is almost essential that the majority of Negro students who are graduated from high school and do not go on to college should be encouraged to attend some kind of a trade or technical school or a vocational school where they can become skilled in specific types of work. Not only their chances of employment, but their opportunities and their chances of staying employed, are increased in proportion to the amount of training they have.

But before the Negro student can decide what type of training is best for him, he needs special help in the choice of a career or occupation, which in turn determines the type of training he would enter. In fact, no amount of vocational guidance is too much for the Negro youth today. His choices at this point very much determine his entire future.

There are many problems involved in helping Negro students plan for the future and decide what seems best for them. The process of selecting a career and preparing for it, and then having the opportunity to enter that field and advance in it, is somewhat different for the Negro young man or woman than it is for the average white student. First, the Negro student has to be convinced that he does have a future; that there is something he can do, and something very worthwhile. Too often, along with his family, he looks upon merely coming through high school as such an accomplishment that it is an end in itself. Most of today's Negro graduates, or at least those with whom I have worked, are the first in their families ever to complete high school. They look upon this achievement as others look upon graduation from college. Then, too, the Negro student has had such a struggle merely to "get through" high school that he has not really been in a position to say with any assurance that he could enter a specific type of training or occupation, or even go to college. What he will make of himself is still more or less a question mark.

Very few Negro children have parents who talk with them in terms of specific careers or occupations, or the importance of going on for more training. No money has been set aside for college or other training. There is no family pattern for the child to follow. The parents are not saying, "I hope you will attend the same college I attended." Or, "There is a business or a job waiting for you." Or, "You can follow in my footsteps," as so many white parents are able to say to their children. The Negro parent can only say, "I hope you won't have to do what I have done all of my life." Yet he is not in a position to offer the child much to implement this wish. The Negro child today is going to have more formal schooling than his parents. And he is going to have to decide very much alone what he does with it. This is not an easy thing for him, because actually he knows so little about the world of work outside menial or domestic jobs that he is not really in a position to decide. He just does not know about the opportunities that do exist. Even the possibility of going to college seems for most Negro students still very remote.

We would say then that the average Negro child has low-level aspirations. This does not mean that he does not want to make something of his life—quite the contrary. He would like to improve his condition more than anything else in the world. But his experiences and his environment have been so limited that he cannot picture himself as holding a major position in the community, or in many different situations. He has never known a Negro scientist, a Negro doctor, a Negro lawyer, a Negro Congressman. The fact that any job would bring in a paycheck and provide food for the table holds considerable attraction for him. He is therefore likely to set his ambitions at a low level, when with preparation and help he might be very capable of performing at a much higher level.

Frequently the abilities and talents of these Negro children, as of other culturally deprived children, are late in developing. Every day we are finding in these children talents and abilities neither we nor they dreamed were there. Sometimes I am absolutely amazed when I think what I have seen in Negro students the last year in high school that I could not see when they entered; or what some are accomplishing in college or on a job that they certainly showed no indication of accomplishing in high school. These students might be said to have "latent talents," that is, talents and abilities which were really there all the time but because of circumstances were not brought to the forefront. And sometimes, but for an unusual experience or a fine teacher, these talents can be smothered to death.

Nathan came to us in the second year of high school. He came about as poorly prepared academically as a boy could be. But Nathan had spirit—that I can say. Perhaps that was his great talent. And if "the spirit can make the master," it certainly did for Nathan. He worked hard, barely passing his courses, even failing a few, and giving no indication of having a gifted mind. One day a young, energetic science teacher, whom Nathan admired very much, called for projects from his students for the Science Fair. Nathan set himself to the difficult task of recording the voices of tiny fishes—so faint, so far, far away that it took the most delicate instruments to detect them. Even then, there were some who doubted the queer sounds were really the voices of fish. Nathan laughed along with them and proved that they were.

The judges lingered when they came to Nathan's project spread out among hundreds on the long tables in the school library. They awarded Nathan a prize for his endeavor and had his picture taken for the newspaper. He was invited to enter his project in a higher division of the Science Fair. It was as if a great breakthrough had taken place in his life. After that, he never seemed to doubt his course. He talked only of going on to college.

Now we began to see what the judges had seen—and what was really there all the time—that Nathan had a keen, inquisitive mind, an analytical creative mind, and a patient way of reasoning things through. These are very good qualities for a man of science—which Nathan is now in the process of becoming. What I am trying to say is that some of these Negro children are truly gifted—how much so, it is difficult to gauge. Their giftedness is often clouded; and it takes unusual experiences to lift those clouds.

More often than not, the selection of a life work is a gradual process dependent upon many factors and many experiences. For this reason, teachers and counselors should begin to talk with the Negro child about his future at an early age, and encourage him to explore many possibilities. There are many ways this can be accomplished. The first, most important step in this process is to get the Negro child to learn as much as he possibly can about himself—his basic personality, his interests, his strengths and weaknesses, his desires. He must ask himself what he expects to get out of life; what activities either in or out of school have given him the most satisfaction; what classes or activities has he excelled in; where has he had the most difficulty.

In finding the answers to these and similar questions about himself, he will need the help of his teachers and counselors, who can tell him much from their observations. They can help him interpret information about himself based on school experiences—grades, achievements, and tests. I would hasten to add, however, that interest, aptitude, and mental-ability tests in their present form should be interpreted with reservations when it comes to Negro students, and never interpreted by persons who are not fully cognizant of their limitations as they apply to culturally deprived children.

Second, this child must begin to learn as much as he can about various careers and opportunities. Since the parents are not often in a position to motivate their children toward new opportunities, it becomes the duty of the school to see that he has access to all kinds of career information, and most importantly, that he knows how to use it. This calls for strong emphasis on career information and opportunities throughout the school years, starting in the lower grades. Of course, such programs are essential today for all children because of new and expanding fields, but most especially so for those children who do not have help at home.

The youngster should select various occupations he thinks he might be interested in or for which he seems to show a talent. He should be helped and encouraged to study and analyze these occupations. He must learn something of the duties involved in these types of work, the training required, the availability and cost of training, opportunities for advancement. What would a career in each of these fields offer, not only at the time he began work, but ten or twenty years later, when his responsibilities are greater? Are these occupations likely to decline in the foreseeable future? How will these fields be affected by automation and technological advances? Is the training required of a nature that it could be applied in other fields as well? And many other things.

In addition to printed information, we can bring to the youngster people from various walks of life who can explain about their work, tell of their experiences, the advantages and disadvantages of their jobs as they see them. The student should be provided an opportunity to talk with these people. It is better still if he can visit them at their work. And he can learn even more if he has a part-time job or a summer job in which he has the opportunity to observe people engaged at the occupation he is interested in. If a girl who wants to be a nurse, for example, can work a summer as an aide in a hospital, she will see firsthand whether she is suited to this type of work.

We know that the interests of a child change from year to year, but we are not sure how much they change. In any event, if in the process of seeking information and learning about careers the student decides a particular occupation is not for him, the effort has served a useful purpose. It is better that he discover this now than later in life.

The student may not be ready to decide at his age on a specific job, but it is helpful if at least he is informed sufficiently to know what general direction he desires to go in—that is, whether he wants to head toward something that will require a college education or some other type of training. The counselor or teacher, insofar as possible, can advise him on the probabilities of success or the risks of failure in his choice. In the end, however, the decision is his alone. No one can make it for him.

The Negro child faces special problems, he needs to know what *his* chances for success are, what opportunities are available to him, *as a Negro*—in business, industry, science, medicine, the trades, and so on. Sometimes it is not just a question of whether he is capable of learning but whether he would be *allowed* to get the basic training required. This is a cold fact, and the children know it. Let me tell you about Donna.

Donna was an attractive Negro girl who stood tall among her classmates. She completed four years of high school in three years. One day a group of nurses came to the school to explain the nurses' training program offered at their hospital. They were dressed in immaculate white uniforms and flowing navy capes. The girls listened eagerly as the women in white described their profession. They emphasized the necessity of devotion to ideals and Christian principles, and a willingness to give a lifetime to others. "It is hard," they said. "If you are not prepared to study and devote your life to others, you need not apply."

The girls listened. So did Donna. Ever since she was a young child, she had said she wanted to be a nurse. We had talked about the requirements of the profession, and now she knew there was more to becoming a nurse than merely wishing. Occasionally she glanced toward me.

When the nurses had finished, the students rushed forward to ask questions. All but Donna. She did not approach the visitors, but turned toward me. "Will they take *me?*" she asked in a low voice.

"Donna," I said, "the good sister has sent word that although they have never had a Negro apply at their school, they have known for a long time that the day would come. They are prepared to accept your application. You must take the same test as the other girls, and the same score will be required of you."

Relief flooded her face. Then, suddenly, it seemed as if she would explode with happiness. "Will you tell my mother?" she said. "Will you tell my mother?" as if a miracle had happened and her mother wouldn't believe it unless the teacher told her.

Here was a young girl with a good mind and gentle ways and a kind heart, who wanted more than anything else to become a nurse. And surely we have need of such people. Yet, until that moment, she had not known whether, *as a Negro,* she would be considered in the training school of her choice. Indeed, I had not known either. That particular school had not accepted a Negro before. Because I knew Donna was interested in that school, I had written beforehand to ask whether she should be encouraged to apply.

The training supervisor had sent the reply by way of the nurses.

The Negro youth of today must be advised not only of his rights but of his opportunities. Rights without opportunities are meaningless. And one need only work for a short while with Negro youngsters in the process of seeking opportunities, to learn how restricted these opportunities are, even today. This is not always because of an institutional policy. The company or the school may have said its doors are open to Negroes. Yet, because of the prejudices of the individuals who actually wield the power, the young Negro may still have a hard time gaining admittance.

The Negro youngster is restricted in his choices in still another way. Discrimination in employment opportunities in the past has limited his range of occupational choices. Those who were able to go into higher training have steered toward teaching and the ministry, for example, because in these fields opportunities were nearly always available on a segregated level. This is why more Negro girls than boys have attended college: the families knew that the girls could always get a job teaching, and if there was any extra money, it was usually spent on the education of the girls. The boys were really not much better off with a college education, because there were few opportunities open to them after they attained it. Even today there are more Negro girls than boys in college. But this is changing; and so it is more urgent than ever that Negro children today be taught to prepare for new occupational patterns.

This summer four of our Negro students working their way through college and other training (Nathan was among them) were employed in one of the world's great scientific laboratories; another boy is employed by the Department of Agriculture. The mother of one of them said, "You know, this couldn't have happened five years ago." And how well I know it. Many times, before the antipoverty programs became popular, I have tried to help Negro youngsters find part-time work in the summer so they could go on to school, and it was practically impossible. The most we could ever get a Negro boy was a job mowing lawns, washing windows, or sweeping out a store at about fifty cents an hour. Looking back, I know that many of these young people never really had a chance. It is no wonder that today they are unemployed, sitting idly on their front porches subsisting on their parents' public-assistance checks.

I find in my experiences with Negro students that there is also an urgent need for strong emphasis on how to look for a job, how to go after one. The social experiences of most Negro youngsters and their contacts with white people in a business way have been so limited that these young people are often at a loss to know how to apply for work. The older students especially need help in how and where to look for a job, methods of application, writing letters of application, how to conduct themselves during an interview, and the importance of manners and appearance. We can help the Negro student by impressing upon him the importance of all these things. If the youngsters do not know how to apply for a job, how to make a good impression during the interview, they may be denied the opportunity to prove themselves.

The student's attitude toward work is a determining factor in his success or failure. More and more employers are saying, "We are willing to take a Negro student and give him a chance, but what about his attitude toward work? Is he dependable? Does he want to learn?" Certainly, we must not overlook the importance of impressing upon these young people as they come out of an age of subservience into one of boundless opportunities that all honest endeavor is worthy. I sometimes get the impression that many of these youngsters are beginning to feel that if they cannot go to college they are doomed to a life of failure. This may stem from the fact that there is such an emphasis on college these days. We must be sure that those students who are not going on to college realize that America still has need of good carpenters, machinists, brickmasons, pipefitters, and even of tillers of the soil. By our example, we must show them that all honest labor is worthy of respect.

The most important thing of all is that the young Negro be encouraged to do what he can do best, what he is the happiest doing. I have never worked with a Negro boy or girl who did not want to make something of his life. Listen again to the children. These are spontaneous statements made by Negro students one day as we sat together and talked about their future.

"I'm going to be a mechanic," said the burly one. "I've always liked to work with cars."

"I'll be a seamstress," said the wiry, quick one. "Already I've won a prize for the best-made dress. Some day I may just have a shop of my own."

"I'd like to be a beautician, and make people pretty."

"I'd like to be a teacher. Do you have to have algebra to be a teacher?"

"And I shall be a secretary and meet people. Do you think I could be a secretary?"

And one, the serious one, who found school easy, waited until the others had spoken. "I haven't decided what I shall do," she said restlessly. "It is very important to me that I help other people."

These children ask so little compared to all this well-endowed nation has to offer its youth. Those with whom I have worked show an unusually high interest in people and groups. They express a desire to teach, go into business, do social work, take up nursing—the service occupations. In the last year or so, I have noticed they are talking of medicine, science, space. No Negro student dared mention such fields ten years ago.

Take David, for example. David is a lanky, thirteen-year-old ninth-grader who first ambled sheepishly through the door of my office last year. "Have you got anything on astronomy?" he asked, referring to the school's career-information file.

"You're interested in astronomy?"

"Uh-huh," he said, and came a step farther.

We got out the "astronomy file." On the cover of one leaflet there was a picture of space and the trail of the Milky Way. Inside were names like Ptolemy, Copernicus, Galileo. David often spends part of his lunch hour studying the information in our files or in the library. He shifts from the astronomy file to the college catalogues. We talk freely now.

While he dreams about big schools where he can meet great teachers and study astonomy, I keep wondering about him and what's going to happen to his dream. From where David and I stand now, the road ahead looks hard indeed. Perhaps I should try to bring him "back to earth" and say something like, "Now, look here, David—your chances of getting to be a great astronomer and going to the type of school you're dreaming about are so remote that you might just as well stop right here and examine yourself and your situation realistically . . ."

But I have seen the sparkle in his eyes when he talks about man's conquest of space. And I have heard him say, "No one in my family ever went to high school. I'm going to high school, and I'm going to college."

The Negro youngster who is able to go on to college is fortunate indeed. It is no wonder that so many Negroes today see a college education as the surest way to defeat both discrimination and poverty. With a college education the Negro is in a position to earn much more during his lifetime. Then, too, there are the personal and intangible benefits of a college education. There is the opportunity to meet and learn to communicate with people of varied backgrounds—which can provide a wonderfully broadening experience for a young Negro. At this age he is by no means a "finished product." He needs more time to grow and stretch his mind in an atmosphere conducive to learning new things about himself and the world in which he lives. While I can think of nothing more wasteful than to push any boy or girl into college who does not belong there, I can think of nowhere else for those who have the desire to go and are capable—where their opportunities for individual fulfillment would be so enlarged.

When Robyn came in the spring to tell me he was ready to choose a college, I was overjoyed, although I knew that finding just the right school for him would be like crossing a mountain barefoot. Robyn was the first of our Negro students to ask to attend an interracial college. He felt that the state university, which had been desegregated for many years, was too large a school for him, considering his background. He wanted a small liberal-arts college where he could take advantage of more individual attention, to strengthen his weak spots. At that time, this meant that we would have to look outside the state. But he did not want to go too far from home because of the extra expense involved in travel, and he wanted to stay in the South.

I had helped hundreds of white students gain admission to colleges all over the country, but I had never helped a Negro seek admission into a predominantly white school. From my association with admissions officers, and from college meetings, etc., I knew a little of the attitudes of many Southern colleges toward Negroes. It seemed very often to be a case of "we'll take you if we are forced to—but we're just hoping you won't apply." I had attended an alumni meeting of one of the so-called great schools of the South; it had crossed my mind that Robyn might be able to make his way there, since I knew this college was heavily endowed and for many years had been showered with funds from the great philanthropic foundations of America. At the meeting I heard the officials apologize to the graduates because they had been forced to integrate the school. They had tried but could no longer hold out in the face of the threatened withdrawal of huge philanthropic grants. The almighty dollar had once more spoken. So, very carefully, it was explained to the graduates that the great school had bowed to the weight of the times and had "recruited" two Negroes. Both, it developed, were older students, one a veteran and the other a housewife. Both lived in town and were part-time day students. The graduates were assured that they would not live in the dormitories. No, this was not the school for Robyn.

There were other enlightening experiences. I found a number of Southern colleges which were looking for one, and only one, Negro student so as to be able to claim that their campuses were desegregated. They wanted a "made-to-order" student, of a certain temperament, with some unusual talent. They seemed to feel that one could reach in a basket and pull out their ideal student. They would say, "Do you have a basketball star or a football star?" Always it was a "star." Some offered to pay all expenses for the "star."

I am sure that Robyn could have gained admittance into any of these schools because of his manner and the ease with which he moved among white people. But I began to wonder what had happened to our ideal of the American college, I wondered if the school is supposed to exist for the benefit of the student, or does the student exist for the convenience of the institution? Of course, I know my range of experiences was limited. But I mention these instances to show a little of what the average Negro student in the South today encounters when he seeks entrance into a predominantly white college. Robyn and I were not looking for just any school so that he could say he had crossed the threshold of a college. We were looking for a good school that would be best for him; and one where he could develop his talents and abilities and not be used as an experiment or a guinea pig.

The selection of a college is of basic importance to any young person. His success or failure may well depend upon his choice. The first step, for the Negro student, is to decide whether he wants to attend a Negro school or a desegregated white school. Most of the Negro youngsters with whom I have worked prefer the predominantly Negro colleges, even after they have attended a desegregated high school. This is in line with national statistics. Approximately eighty percent of the Negroes now in college are attending the 123 Negro colleges in America, 119 of which are in the South. The majority of these students seems to prefer the Negro college because of the more natural social life. They feel more at ease among their own people. They can participate in all extra-curricular activities, become campus leaders, and belong to fraternities and sororities. Many expect to meet their future husband or wife in college.

There are many advantages to the segregated Negro college. I feel that there will be a great need for these colleges for some time to come, and actually that many Negro students may be better off in the Negro college, not only for the reasons mentioned, but because the programs of instruction are more often suited to their academic achievements. These schools have served the most poverty-stricken students from the poorest states and from the weakest segregated public schools for so many years that they are familiar with the problems of the Southern Negro. They have developed special courses and ways of working with this type of student.

I have never had a Negro student turned away from a Negro college, even though his school record was weak. If he was capable of grasping even elementary college work and indicated that he was ready to do his part, he was given every opportunity. The choice, of course, depends upon the individual student and what he feels is best for him.

The chief problem in the selection of a college arises when the Negro youngster chooses to attend a predominantly white college. Although most of these are now desegregated at least in token, the Negro student is far from feeling at ease on many desegregated campuses of the South. In many cases he may be among the very first Negroes to attend the white college. This places him under a certain stress. He becomes somewhat of a spectacle. Frequently there is considerable publicity and perhaps even hostility.

If the youngster prefers an interracial school, the questions that arise are: Where can he find the courses best suited to his needs and ambitions—in a small or a large school? Where would he stand academically in the freshman class? Is the academic achievement of the freshman class as a whole so high that he would be lost in his courses? How has the particular college received Negroes in the past? How has the community looked upon Negroes in the college? Will he be able to walk downtown and sit at a lunch counter or attend a movie, or will he be virtually imprisoned on the campus?

After some preliminary research, Robyn and I decided to call upon the National Scholarship Service and Fund for Negro Students for help on these many questions. We found this organization of inestimable aid. The NSSFNS is a non-profit agency directed by outstanding educators, college presidents, and private citizens. Its aim is to provide free advisory service to qualified Negro students. In the past fifteen years this agency has helped over ten thousand Negro youngsters gain admission to, and obtain financial aid and employment in, over 350 interracial colleges. With the assistance of the high school the youngster has attended, the Service considers his abilities, interests, and financial situation, and if he is qualified recommends to him several colleges that seem best suited to his needs, colleges

175

where he would be considered for admission and where he would be able to obtain aid if he needs it.

The NSSFNS recommended three colleges to Robyn. All three are small schools noted for quality training and are in communities not hostile to minority groups. We now knew the schools where his application would receive serious consideration, and where he would not be embarrassed by making application. This was our first big hurdle. The next step would be to qualify for entrance. The Service can only recommend schools. The student must meet the entrance requirements, which vary from school to school.

Robyn began the long process of filling in seemingly endless papers. There were financial statements to be prepared by his parents. They, too, needed help with the complicated forms. Here Robyn's mother was very helpful. She would go as far as she could in the application, and then we would have a long telephone conversation. There were recommendations too. By now Robyn had proved himself and had won the respect not only of the students and the teachers but of many influential white citizens. They all wanted to help in some way. No boy ever applied for college entrance from our school with higher or more genuine recommendations.

Then came the tests. Robyn went to one town to take the College Board Examinations, to another for the American College Test, and one school sent tests to the high school. When he had finished, he was not jubilant. He saw how much he did not know and had had no way of knowing. One test, for example, contained a section on geography. Robyn had not had a geography class since the early grades. On another test there were many questions involving problems in government—which in our school would not be covered in class until the last semester of high school. One college asked for a "writing sample." Although he had improved greatly in composition writing, it was still very weak. We knew that unless the colleges took his background into account, we faced a serious setback.

Robyn was only one of the vast number of Negroes who, having come from inferior segregated schools in the South, found himself less prepared for these tests than most white students. The fault is not so much with the tests as with the poor preparation of the Negro student. Even though these youngsters may have come twice as far as the average white student, considering where they were at the time they entered the white high school, they are very likely to find themselves still behind the average white applicant. This brings into question the validity of the standard college-entrance tests, as well as other tests, as an accurate measure of the potential of students from deprived backgrounds. There are obviously many limitations to these tests which should be especially taken into account in reference to Negro children.

Practically all college-entrance tests rate one's academic achievement in two or more basic subjects. The degree of achievement shown will depend in large measure on the courses a student has had in high school, always on the excellence of his training, and, of course, on his own scholastic competence as well. These tests are intended as predictive measures of success in college. But there are a great many intangible, yet highly important factors involved which may well provide the nucleus of a successful college career or life and which these tests cannot possibly predict. They do not show creative, artistic, or leadership abilities; they cannot measure human kindness or concern for one's fellow man; courage or endurance; ambition and drive—human forces so powerful they defy measurement.

We recognize the many advantages of testing. However, the danger in relying solely on tests in providing opportunities for culturally deprived children is not in the tests themselves but in how the tests are used. When test results are examined in the light of other information such as school background, grades in school, recommendations of teachers, personal qualities of the student, they can be very helpful. The danger arises when schools use specific scores within a close range as cut-off points for admission and scholarships or work opportunities, and give little consideration to anything else. I am sorry to say I have found some colleges where this is done. If the student's score is a fraction below the cut-off point, he may be denied admission or denied aid without which he cannot enter.

We know from various follow-up studies that the Negro is likely to achieve better in college than the entrance examinations indicate. I have seen this myself. In fact, even the best-prepared Negro students from our school have never made more than a low-average score on these tests, and some have been honor students in college.

When we rely solely on tests for the selection of students, we are placing ourselves in a position of casting the youth of America as one would grade products in a market. Are the advantages so great that the nation can afford the errors? I feel strongly that youngsters like Robyn and others from disadvantaged backgrounds who have a potential, however clouded it may be in the early days, should be out of the reach of "technicians" and in the hands of people of vision who are able to see purpose and meaning to a life beyond what can be classified in a machine.

We were very fortunate that Robyn had fallen into such hands. In April of his last year, word came that he had been accepted by Berea College, one of the great schools in America. Berea is a small college in the mountains of eastern Kentucky. It was established and exists mainly for the children of Appalachia, who otherwise could not afford a college education. Its doors are never closed to any boy or girl from the mountain region who has a genuine desire to learn and is willing to work. At Berea, all the students work to help earn their way.

I knew that Robyn's talents would be nourished here, that he would grow and develop in the wonderful atmosphere of the institution, helped by the dedicated people under whom he would study. They had not considered the color of his skin, or whether he was a "star." They had seen a boy with potential who needed help. His test scores were low, as we had expected. It was recommended that he begin in the summer school immediately after graduation from high school. There he could work to make up his deficiencies. It all seemed too good to be true.

Shortly afterwards, word came that the National Scholarship Service and Fund for Negro Students, through its Supplementary Scholarship Fund, had provided $400 for Robyn's expenses the first year. Although he would earn a part of his way with work at the school, he still needed a few hundred dollars to see himself securely through the first year. The money he had saved would now have to go for summer school. Here was our last big hurdle. But then a man-made miracle happened.

While Robyn was in summer school and I was wondering where the last few dollars, which seemed like a million now, would possibly come from, a very special airmail letter containing a handsome check came to my desk. The letter was from a prominent citizen, a retired businessman and author who was now living in California. "My wife and I want you to use this," he wrote, "to help a worthy Negro student."

And now, our cup ran over. I wrote the giver and told him of Robyn and asked if he would approve sending the check on to the college for Robyn. He was delighted. And this was the beginning of a long and close friendship between a great American citizen and a black boy from the mountains of Tennessee—each of whom has a desire by direct action to make America a better place in which to live. The great philanthropist gave more than money. He gave his heart. He wrote Robyn letters of encouragement. He kept up with his accomplishments in school. He never forgot to congratulate Robyn on every achievement. He was very pleased when Robyn played basketball at the college.

Robyn has been an honor student. The college representatives never come from Berea that they do not mention how proud the school is of his fine example of citizenship and of his accomplishments—and those of his brother, who is now well on his way toward the study of medicine. Many people worked together to make Robyn's entrance into college a reality. He and all the others like him must have help, and help of many kinds and from many sources. Each person can only do so much or go so far. Where one leaves off, another must take up.

There are many ways the colleges of America can help the Negro student. They are helping more every day. Many colleges have set up planned programs to take a certain number of disadvantaged students and provide special tutorial services, remedial classes, special counseling. With the aid of funds provided by the federal government under recent legislation, and funds from other sources, many colleges are bringing high-school youngsters to their campuses during the summer and providing special help in reading, mathematics, and other subjects. They are sending college students into the rural and slum areas to work with disadvantaged students and help prepare them for college. Many admissions officers are actively scouting the country for talented students. They talk with youngsters when they visit the high schools, invite them to the campus, let them know they are interested. The Cooperative Admission and Aid Plan established only recently by the Association of College Admissions Counselors is an outstanding example of this trend.

Under this plan, a number of colleges have agreed to consider for admission, with the promise of aid, a number of especially referred youngsters. The candidates, of course, would have to meet admission requirements; but it would be expected that test scores and other objective data would be interpreted in light of the students' backgrounds. After the student's acceptance, the college helps further by providing employment or financial aid, help in adjusting to college life, tutorial services if needed, assistance for travel home at holidays or in case of family emergencies. To my mind, this is what it has to come to, and on a much larger scale.

It is not enough for colleges to say, "Our doors are open if you qualify." Or, "Our doors are open if you have the money." Few Negro students will qualify at present, as white students of middle-class families might be expected to qualify. But the doors of the colleges of America should not be closed to them. In another decade perhaps we can expect the Negro students to be more nearly "even" with white students. By then they will have had the training, the cultural experiences, a better standard of living which will make this possible. But, meanwhile, what happens to those students in school now who have not had these advantages and who do have good minds and can learn and want to go on? Are they to be crippled the rest of their lives?

The colleges of America have the same responsibility toward disadvantaged youngsters, both black and white, as those of us in the public high schools. The colleges, too, exist for and because of the youth of America. Because we must take these students as they are and wherever they are, the colleges are going to have to have flexible admission requirements. If the schools of higher education do not share with us the responsibility of providing special help for these students, a whole generation of young Negroes will never be able fully to realize their potentialities.

Every year now, the number of Negro students working toward a college education has increased, until this past year in our school more than fifty percent of the Negro graduates expressed a desire to enter college. All of them were not able to do so in September, mainly for financial reasons. But they are working to save money or completing their time in the armed services with this goal in mind.

Lincoln, a Negro boy who was graduated from high school a year ago and is now serving with a missile battalion in the artillery, provides a typical example. Lincoln wanted more than anything to attend college. There were so many obstacles that he decided to volunteer for the army before trying to go on. After a year in the Service, he has not given up his ambition.

"Lately, I've been doing a lot of thinking about myself, my future, and the responsibilities I will be faced with," he writes. "I do want to make something of myself. I realize it will take a lot of hard work but I want to work toward setting a goal for my life. I am not afraid of responsibility which I am faced with . . ." He goes on to tell how he is taking college courses by correspondence while in the Service.

Thus, one can see, the level of these children's aspirations has been raised by their experiences in desegregation. Helping them channel their abilities and dreams is like exploring a new land—vastly rewarding and full of inestimable riches.

❀❖❀❖❀❖❀❖❀❖❀❖❀❖❀

8

Cast Down Your Bucket

Any great social movement calls for various kinds of actions and personalities. There are those who envision a new land and cross the mountains to find it. Then there are those who come after them. They cut down the forests, build the homes, plow the good earth, and plant the seeds. They nourish the soil, reap the harvest, and conserve it for future generations. The first are the dreamers and the pioneers who dare to be different and brave the hardships. The ones who come after are the builders who take up where the pioneers leave off. They mold, strengthen, and preserve. In the affairs of men there is a time for each.

During the past decade, the Negro leaders have pioneered and made it possible for the Negro in America to "grow up." They have led the marches and the demonstrations. Their prayers have been heard around the world, and not without considerable embarrassment to this nation. They have performed a great service to America. They have forced us to take a close look at ourselves and our national objectives. They have aroused the conscience of a people. They have brought about the enactment of new laws and the repeal of archaic laws, so that all men can be free. The time now approaches for different types of leadership and actions.

At some point the turmoil must cease and the Negro must begin to direct his energies toward cementing the gains, as in war we begin to prepare for a lasting peace. The Negro must now begin to look to an age which will be vastly different from the time just past—an age in which he will develop and utilize his talents. The talents of his race are relatively untapped. I like to think that the new age will be one of diplomacy and statesmanship, an "age of achievement." Unless this age is forthcoming, it is possible that he will have lost many of his gains.

In this new age he must begin to speak for himself as an individual and accept the responsibility for his own destiny. The new way of life must come from him. It cannot be imposed upon him. Laws can only make it possible. When he is able to speak for himself as an individual and show attainment as an individual, he will move as a people into the new age of achievement. This will be his "finest hour."

If there is any one word which might describe my plea to the young Negro today and in the days ahead, I think perhaps it would be the word "responsibility." One way of looking at it, we can give the young Negro everything he asks for and more; and at the same time, if we do not prepare him for the acceptance of responsibility which accompanies freedom and opportunity, we have failed both him and ourselves.

I suppose we all have words that call to mind certain experiences. The word "responsibility" does that for me. In 1964 Dr. Charles Gomillion, noted educator and sociology professor at Tuskegee Institute in Alabama, asked me if I would come to Tuskegee and talk to the twelve Negro youngsters who had weathered the first year of desegregation there. When Dr. Gomillion told me something of these children and their ordeals, I felt I could not refuse, although it was with much apprehension that I made the trip.

The Tuskegee High School was ordered desegregated by a federal court order in 1963. In September of 1963 the city complied with the court order, and the twelve Negro children entered the school. At that time the governor of the state ordered the school closed and sent a national-guard unit to enforce his order. President Kennedy immediately federalized the guardsmen and the school was opened. Then all the white pupils joined in a boycott of the school. From late fall until December, the remainder of the first semester, the twelve Negro children sat alone in a school building designed for 250 pupils. The thirteen white teachers in the school were so loyal that they refused to leave their jobs, and stayed with the Negro children.

In January, the Alabama Board of Education ordered the school closed. The Negro children were then divided into two groups and sent to previously segregated high schools in towns ten and twenty miles away. Thereupon these schools were also boycotted by the white pupils. A private school was set up in the county for the white students. In April, one of the schools which the Negro children attended was partially burned down. But the Negro children, ranging in age from thirteen to eighteen, completed the year. Three were graduated.

At the end of the year, in June, the Negro citizens of the community decided to have a special program honoring the twelve children who had endured the year. Tension was still very high in the community, and in the entire region for that matter; and I really did not know what to expect.

It was on a Sunday morning that we drove the last forty miles of the journey from Columbus, Georgia, to Tuskegee. The narrow asphalt roads wound through desolate, poor countryside in the heart of the Black Belt, known for its great cotton plantations in bygone times. The day was so hot that only occasionally did we see someone outside. Just before noon, we came to the little town of Tuskegee. We drove to the edge of the town to the beautiful campus of Tuskegee Institute. The grounds are interspersed with spruce and hemlock, tall pine trees, and age-old magnolias. It was like reaching an oasis in a desert.

Here we saw the neat homes of the professors, which had been constructed mainly with student labor—even the concrete blocks were made on the campus—and the quaint museum, at the foot of a grassy hillside, in which are housed the experiments and mementos of the great scientist George Washington Carver, one of Tuskegee's early teachers. We saw also the pottery shop, the industrial shops, the nursing school, the veterinary school, and the veterans hospital, which, ironically, houses more whites than Negroes. All about us there was evidence of creativity and ingenuity—no doubt a carry-over from the days of Booker T. Washington, the school's first president, who held an abiding faith that people should do for themselves.

After refreshments and rest at the Dorothy Gray Guest House on the campus, we went to the little red-carpeted Greenwood Baptist Church, which was filled to capacity. It was now three o'clock in the afternoon. By now the big Sunday meals are cooked and served, the dishes done. The kitchen shades have been drawn. And now, even as in the old days, the Negroes know that the remainder of the day

187

belongs to them. They rush home to discard the aprons and the white coats, and bedeck themselves in the "Sunday go-to-meetin'" clothes. Then, one by one, they ease down to the pews—mothers and fathers, aunts and uncles, grandmothers and grandfathers. There is no place in all the world so sacred to a Southern Negro as his own little church.

There were many white people in the audience that day, including some of the white teachers who had stayed in the classrooms with the twelve children. They looked tired and worn from their year's experience. Members of the school board came, and ministers of many denominations—some from as far away as Montgomery. I saw in all of these people a genuine desire to find workable solutions to their racial difficulties.

The twelve Negro children sat in the front row. The girls wore white dresses. The boys had on white shirts and ties, and coats, despite the heat. The parents of many of these children held doctor's degrees. Some were professors at the Institute. The children were well-reared, mannerly, and intelligent. It seemed inconceivable that anyone would try to prevent such children from receiving a proper education or would object to attending classes with them.

Dr. Gomillion, a native South Carolinian who has devoted his life to securing equal opportunities for his people, said, in his soft-spoken way, "We want you to say anything you want to. We want our children to hear different views and opinions from many people." The dean of women expressed much the same view. Amid this gracious atmosphere and the wonderful hospitality of these people, both black and white, who had seen so much trouble, I felt free to speak from my heart.

188

What does one say to Negro youth today? What should we be saying to them, conditions being what they are? I could only think that youth's place in our history must never be to tear down or destroy, but only to build. And in order to build, one must start with oneself. There are few now who doubt the freedom the Negro has worked so hard to gain is well within sight. The majority of today's Negro children will never know the injustices suffered by their grandparents or even by their parents. They will never know what it means not to be able to receive a proper education, not to be able to vote, or to be referred to as a person having only "half a soul," as was the custom in some parts of the South in the old days. These things belong to a social order that is wholly inadequate for life in the twentieth century. The freedom today's Negro children will know carries tremendous responsibilities. Are we all fully aware of those responsibilities?

And so, that hot summer afternoon in a little Negro church in Alabama, while the women fanned themselves with the programs, we forgot the dreadful past. We looked to the future, which belongs to youth. We talked of the young Negro's responsibilities in this new "age of achievement." I could not see these boys and girls as twelve individuals who had endured a terrible year: they were representatives of the Negro children with whom I had been so closely associated, and of all the Negro children of the South. It had been my greatest hope that whatever I might be able to say to them would apply to all Negro youth. There is now an imperative need for more constructive direction among Negro youth, and for less radical leadership than that to which they have been exposed in recent months. Later it was the proudest moment of my life when the government asked to use our talk of that afternoon in the overseas "Voice of America" broadcasts. I could never recapture the intense mood or the spirit of those people in the little church that day, but I can tell you a few of the things we discussed.

The first is that the young Negro must develop himself so that he can be a useful citizen. The perpetuation of a democratic society such as ours depends upon the knowledge, the good judgment, and the wisdom of all the people. After his civil rights are realized, as they are being realized, the young Negro must have something to offer the society of which he is now a part. His most important task at this time, therefore, is to stay in school, whether it be a segregated or a desegregated school, and get as much education as he possibly can. For education is the key to his future.

He must read and study, and study and read more. He must never feel that he has acquired so much knowledge that he does not need any more. Education is never completed. There is no point in today's world when anyone of us can say, "I have arrived. I have learned all there is to learn or all I need to know."

In addition, he must educate himself to cope with the one known certainty: change. We cannot tell him what the world will be like a quarter of a century from now, or what the mind of man will conceive. A job today is no longer something most people can prepare for and reasonably expect to hold or to perform in the same manner the rest of their lives. We must all be prepared to accept change—change necessitated by accelerated technological advances and an exploding population—the results of which no one can predict. Even with a good education, there is a strong possibility that many young people of

190

today will have to be retrained at some time in the future. And it is difficult to retrain a person who cannot read or write, as we are finding with many of the displaced coal miners in the Southern mountains.

Some young Negroes will ask, as I have heard Negro students ask, "How can I get an education when the schools are so inadequate, when I have no place to study, when there is no one in my family to help me, when I don't have money to buy the things the other boys and girls have, when my own parents don't even care what happens to me—when I feel lonely and unwanted?" This may indeed be so, and these conditions will not be erased overnight. The children of today are affected by them. We must face them together in their ugliness. Some of the personal problems facing Negro youngsters are almost insurmountable. At the same time, there is more hope now for the Negro than ever before. Because of increased opportunity, there is really no time now for the young Negro to use these handicaps as an excuse. If he does, he is doomed. He is going to have to work mightily to overcome them; but he can do it, and must. His commitments with the future depend on how he prepares himself today. Even a long history of deprivation can be offset—not simply by having doors opened, but by strenuous effort on the part of the young Negro.

Today's young Negro must make up his mind that he will not lay down his life as another link in the chain of ignorance and poverty. The future holds too much hope. Right now he must set himself to the things in his life that are important and will count the most later. This is not just for himself, but as part of his obligation to those who will come after him. Because of the nature of the times and the issues involved, every young Negro today is setting an example. If one in a family or a neighborhood can come through high school, others will know it is possible for them. If one can enter college, others know there is a chance for them also. If one can get a good job, others will not lose hope.

Second, the young Negro must never forget that he is first a citizen of America, a natural-born citizen, with the same responsibilities as every other citizen to protect the principles upon which this nation was founded. And if, amid our racial strife, he feels inclined to think unkindly of the American way of accomplishing change, he might remember that nowhere else in the world can grievances be aired so freely as here. And in spite of the history of the Negro here, American democracy has produced the largest group of outstanding Negroes in the world—from the colonial poet Phillis Wheatley to two Nobel Peace Prize winners in recent years, Dr. Ralph Bunche and the Reverend Martin Luther King.

The nation has at last recognized the injustice of slavery and deprivation, and is moving on an unprecedented scale to alleviate these conditions. No nation in the world in all history has expended more effort or more money, or endured more bloodshed, in trying to right a wrong. And despite the past, and even present conditions, nowhere in the world are the children better clothed, better fed, better cared for than right here. Nowhere else is the standard of living higher—even for the Negro.

I find this very difficult to explain to foreign exchange students. It seems, no sooner they arrive, than they want to know about the "Negro problem." It is obvious from their questions that our racial problems have been used around the world to castigate the principles for which this nation stands. I try to explain that we know conditions are not what we would like them to be, not only for the Negroes but for one fifth of our population who are poor and deprived; and that we are working to correct these injustices, that we are making progress, that it will take time.

I remember a German boy who came to our school who seemed to have the idea that in America we spent our time persecuting Negroes and made a practice of "killing" them. He was prepared to help defend them. He was here during the terrible turmoil in Birmingham, and he wanted to go to Birmingham and help. I had a very hard time convincing him that he was not here to become involved in our racial struggle.

After a year here, he did finally concede that there are many sides to the Negro's struggle in America which he had not realized before he came. In one of our last conversations before he left for New York, he said, "I understand more now why things are as they are."

I have heard young Negroes say, "We are beginning to realize our strength . . . We have gotten bigger than America. We look at the African history. We have gotten so we claim Africa."

Once, a long time ago, in 1817, the American Colonization Society was formed for the primary purpose of sending the Negroes back to Africa. This movement was supported by benevolent slaveowners who wanted to make amends for something they knew was wrong. A tract of land on the western shores of Africa was chosen and named "Liberia," meaning "land of freedom." In 1820, eighty-six Negro immigrants left New York City for their new home in Africa—for freedom. But on their arrival, some refused to unload their baggage and returned with the ship. A few remained, but the project was doomed to failure not just because of epidemics and lack of funds, but mainly because of the attitudes of the Negroes themselves. The American Negro has always shown great loyalty to his country. In every war he has fought side by side with the white soldier. In the deepest poverty and despair he has rejected radicalism; it is this time-tested loyalty to America and its institutions which has brought a nation to bow in humility.

Negroes have a right to air their grievances. It is better in many ways that grievances be aired than suppressed. And fine people everywhere have helped the Negro in his protests. But the burden of complaint, to my mind, should be borne by responsible Negro and white adults of the community who are old enough to weigh experiences and situations and who know the dangers of a revolutionary atmosphere. The young Negro, as I see it, has so much to do and so far to go that he does not have the time to take to the streets. He can be of true help to his people by concentrating on developing and improving himself.

I would suggest also that the young Negro must face the fact that he is in a minority, that he constitutes a little over one tenth of the population of the nation. Any minority group in any country must have the cooperation of the majority in order to live peacefully and successfully. While it is basic in our society that all people be heard and their welfare considered, there are some things that laws cannot provide, even though it took the laws to put the country on the right course in the first place. The young Negro is still going to need more than new laws. Laws cannot force people to be friends. They cannot force people to be good neighbors. These are privileges that individuals acquire out of mutual respect and consideration for one another. Respect must be earned. It is not likely that it will grow out of a continued unrest, out of torn communities. As a young Negro boy said, "There's not but one way now for us to get what we want. That is through educating ourselves and gaining the respect of white people. We have got to have their respect to get anywhere. We aren't going to get their respect by ruining their businesses."

Despite the bitterness that surrounds this struggle, the young Negro must not permit himself to become intolerant. When he does, he falls victim to the same type of prejudice and racism of which radical whites are guilty. It will take strength on his part to remain tolerant. And here again, education is of the greatest importance. As we improve our ability to communicate, we grow in our understanding of one another.

I have heard young Negroes in the streets boast: "We know just what to say to the white man. We tell him just what he wants to hear—no more. After he's gone, we laugh about what we said to him." Perhaps the white man in the South has never really understood the Negro and the deep feelings he must have borne these many years. But the white man is now in the process of trying to understand and trying to help. He, too, is being challenged to a new way of life, and it takes time to consolidate understanding, which is essential to change. The Negro has an obligation to do his part in helping to bring about better understanding, which ultimately will produce a change in the attitudes of the white man.

On Memorial Day, 1963, at Gettysburg, Lyndon Johnson said, "In this hour, it is not our respective races which are at stake—it is our nation. Let those who care for their country come forward, North and South, white and Negro, to lead the way through this moment of challenge and decision. The Negro says, 'Now.' Others say, 'Never.' The voice of responsible Americans—the voice of those who died here and of the great man who spoke here—their voices say, 'Together.' There is no other way."

As the young Negro pulls himself up, he has a moral obligation to help those of his own race less fortunate or less endowed. I find that many young Negroes today feel this obligation very deeply. A Negro boy said, "I plan to study for two careers—one to make a living, and I also want to study some kind of social work so I can help my people." Many Negro youngsters in high school teach a Sunday School class, help with a teen-age group, or, on their own, talk with other young Negro students who might need help. One Negro girl quit school and then returned because she had been influenced by another girl who talked with her about the importance of finishing school.

This concern for the welfare of others is most encouraging. For as the young Negro begins to feel a responsibility to help his own people, he will become more involved in other aspects of American life where his help is needed. And, certainly, we can use all the help we can get, for the racial problem is only one of many critical problems facing America today.

Only recently, for example, in a conversation with a university professor, I discussed the many great improvements that could come with the anti-poverty programs; surely now, if we work hard, the plight of the Southern Negro can be improved. "And have you thought," he said, "that actually about three fourths of the people who can benefit by these programs are the poor whites in our own Appalachia?" There are many distressed areas here, with problems not unlike those of the Negro. Conditions in Appalachia may be due to different causes, but the results have been the same: a debasement of mankind. Here, in these beautiful mountains, too many of our children have become the victims of inadequate schools, inadequate job opportunities, ignorance, and apathy.

A friend of mine, one of the fine craftsmen of the area, who lives with his family on a mountaintop in Georgia, wrote: "Our mountain, like many mountains, is rotten in all the ways man can find to cause things to decay. We have an empty school building crowning our mountaintop. Our unemployment rate in this county is over sixteen percent. We have only one lawyer in the county, only one doctor. We have trash heaps on our highways and commercialism (poverty of spirit) ruining and eating up our best resources: nature's creation. It is grim.

"The discouraging realities of every day in the Southern mountains are overwhelming . . . But we have tremendous faith that there can be worked out the best solutions to all of these problems."

Solutions are at hand. As the passage of civil-rights legislation in 1964 and of the Voting Rights Bill in 1965 are major steps in easing conditions for the Negro, so the anti-poverty programs will help rejuvenate the mountain areas. We will have new roads, new schools, reforestation, water-control, and clean-up projects. These are good things and must come.

And with these improvements something else must come. It must follow after the conscience of a people has been aroused. It is as necessary for the war against discrimination as it is for the war against poverty, as important for the Negro as for ourselves. It is what I like to call "an integrity of spirit"—what my friend on the mountaintop has, what our forebears had. It means faith in ourselves, faith to face the state of things as they are, and to do the things that must be done; faith to know that in America there are sensible ways and means to accomplish all necessary tasks. It means to think big and to dream big, to buckle down and work, to help your neighbor and your neighbor's children. Together, and only together, can we break this cycle of ignorance, poverty, and prejudice, so that every person in America can achieve his own individual greatness.

And, in the end, I would hope that as the young Negro grows older, he would think seriously before leaving the South. We know conditions here are not what they should be, but we have also seen that they are little better elsewhere. When the Negro leaves the South, he usually migrates to the great cities of the East or the North. But just now few of these people are really prepared to cope with life in the cities. The great metropolises are already burdened with mammoth problems in housing, crime, unemployment, with problems arising from segregation, and so on. The Southern Negro only contributes to these problems, which even now seem almost insoluble.

There are other reasons. The South is the home of the Negro. His roots are here. He is a part of the green hills and the black earth, the fabulous and leisurely living, the bloodshed, of the old days; and a part of the machines and the industries of the new world. The folk songs, stories, art, even the dialect of the American Negro are deeply engrained in our way of life. And not all of this has been unkind.

I have faith that in "a few more days" home will be a better place. It is a better place right now. By facing our problems on home ground rather than running away from them or transferring them to another section of the country, we not only help the nation as a whole, but we bring stature to the South. Booker T. Washington had a valuable contribution to make on this subject in his address at the opening of the Atlanta Exposition in 1895. He stressed that the solutions to our racial problems will come from ourselves, that no one can provide them for us. He told the story of a ship lost at sea which eventually sighted a friendly vessel. The distressed ship signaled, "Water, water; we die of thirst!" The friendly ship answered back, "Cast down your bucket where you are." Then a second signal came from the distressed ship: "Water, water; send us water!" And again the friendly vessel replied, "Cast down your bucket where you are." More signals passed back and forth, until eventually the distressed ship heeded the friendly vessel's request. The captain cast down his bucket, and it came up full of fresh, sparkling water from the mouth of the Amazon River.

And Washington went on: "To those of my race who depend on bettering their condition in a foreign land, or who underestimate the importance of cultivating friendly relations with the Southern white man, who is their next-door neighbor, I would say, 'Cast down your bucket where you are—cast it down in making friends in every manly way of the people of all races by whom we are surrounded.' "

9

Out of My Heart

A^ND now it is spring again. Contrary to Nature's plan, spring is the time of harvest for a schoolteacher. One looks back and thinks of all that should have been done and could have been done, and realizes how little was ever really accomplished in comparison. It is in perspective that one can see the real, more lasting progress. And while there were many setbacks in working with the Negro children, and no doubt there will be for a long time, I could now begin to see the little, everyday changes in both the children and ourselves which in the end, hopefully, may make a vast difference.

Although I never cease to recognize how difficult the road ahead is for many of these children, as well as for ourselves, I have never lost faith that in due time, if not they, then their children, would be able to stand up before all the world and say, "I have my place under the sun. I am a decent human being, and I accept my responsibilities as a free citizen in a free country."

I do not know how anyone could work with these children day by day and hear and see the yearnings that must be theirs, and the quiet courage with which they endure, and not become involved in some way in trying to improve their plight—if for no other reason than to cleanse his own conscience. On my desk there is a glass top. The children who come into my office often press their hands against the glass top as they sit and talk—the way Robyn did that day, and Annie, and others. And sometimes by the end of the day there are hundreds of smudged fingerprints quite noticeable. Usually I take a damp cloth and wipe the smudges away in preparation for each new day. But often, as I do, I think back to the children who sat there during the day and pressed their hands against the top, reaching inside themselves, and outside too, for a new day and a new world. And no matter how many voices I can hear jumbled and close up and far away, one thing stands above all else. Even in despair, they echo hope and courage—the most human of all qualities and the qualities that guarantee all others. Listen once more to the children and then cover your ears if you can:

"The only thing I know is maybe it will be easier for someone else."

"If Bobby can do it, I can too."

"We're coming—slowly but surely we're coming."

"I want to be a beautician and make people pretty."

"No one in my family ever went to high school. I'm going to high school, and I'm going to college."

And on and on—

And sometimes, as I wipe away the smudged fingerprints, I think how wonderful it would be if we could erase the distorted thoughts from our minds, and the hatreds of three hundred years, and begin to mold a new generation free of mental slavery. What a wonderful generation that would be.

And while these children have taxed my limited knowledge with the endless questions they have posed, and have brought me heartaches sometimes, and even tears, the warmth of their friendship has filled the rooms as we have shared new ventures together. They have taught me a little of what I had to know about myself, about the South, and about America.

Victoria will stand beside me the longest day I live. For it took Victoria to teach the teacher what prejudice and hate can mean and what man can do to man. In her hurt and in her innocence she could see ahead a hundred years. Through her tears she spoke the truth. And I know now she spoke the truth; and I am indebted to her. I never work with a Negro child who has succeeded that I don't think back to Victoria and how she helped to make that child's success possible because she "endured."

Some days, near winter especially, Victoria comes to see me and we go into my attic and pick out the discarded children's clothes—the coats and shoes, the baby blankets and toys, for her little ones. She tells me how smart they are.

"You must read them stories, Victoria," I tell her, "lots and lots of stories, and send them to the Head Start programs so they will be ready for school."

"Oh, yes, ma'am, I do," she said.

And Robyn would stand in front of all of us. He was the wise one with the strength of the hills in his soul and yet he walked on tiptoes. There is no doubt in my mind that one day you will hear from this young man, and from others who are moving on.

Roberta, my child who had waited for books, promised to come back to school one day. We would not give up—not yet anyway—not ever really. Sometimes, some things are just too much for one lifetime, and they have to go down again and come out somewhere else. Maybe the beautiful, youthful dreams she folded and put away will come out again in her children. I hope and pray that they will, and that the world will be more receptive and kinder. For each of us is weaker today because the spirit of this child was crushed.

Others are going on to do many things—good things. There is one very tall black boy who will be a brickmason. I can see him now holding his trowel and mortar proudly. Because his dream is my dream also, I would journey far indeed to see his first building. And who knows, maybe one day David will be the great astronomer he talked about. If he should be, one starry night a little part of me will travel to the planets with him. This realization is the wonder and the glory of it all.

Then there have been the small, simple things that touch the heart—the Christmas card this year from Vietnam with a scribbled note at the bottom, "Thanks for everything." And the special invitation to Annie's wedding at the little church "on the hill." When we arrived that rainy summer evening, Annie's mother instructed the usher to seat us "up front" with the family. And there is a Negro boy who clerks at a chain grocery. He knows how hurriedly and carelessly I choose my groceries. When I take a head of lettuce or a melon that is not too good, he will ease over and whisper, "You don't want that." And off he runs to the basement of the big store to pry the lid off a new crate.

How I wish I could wait for their children and see the difference there is bound to be. But I am proud to have been a part of their first step in the "thousand-mile journey." Already I have seen enough to know that they will be able to teach their children a little better because they have been taught. This will make all the difference. And always I hope that they will spread knowledge and skill, but also matters of the heart and soul, so the world can be a better place than they found it. We never talked about what the country could do for them without discussing what they could do for their country.

Granted the opportunity, these children are ready to help us refashion our suspicious and untidy world. Hope is written on all their faces. All over the South today Negro children are hitching their wagons to stars. And if you join them in their journey, you'll find you feel a little closer to God.

To my mind, the task of educating the Negro children of the South as they should be educated is an unpaid debt of the twentieth century in which we each owe a part. It is a staggering debt. And yet, in an age when man can conceive of nothing he might not invent, it seems almost inconceivable that we would not look upon our responsibility to these children and this new era as a time of great challenge.

Of all the people who are in a position to encourage and help the Negro children of the South and protect their rights and secure their opportunities, the American public-school teacher is the most important. A teacher—a real teacher—can fling a thread across a chasm of the mind of a child and build a bridge that will last to all eternity.

Only recently, I visited a Negro elementary school far back in the mountains of east Tennessee. There a middle-aged Negro teacher, whom I shall call "Anna," waits with a younger teacher in a dilapidated two-room school with twenty-five Negro children in grades one through eight. Last year there were forty children who attended the school. A week before school began this past fall, Anna did not know how many of the children would return. She did not even know whether she would have a job. The county maintains a "freedom of choice" policy—that is, the Negro children can go to the white school or they can stay in the segregated school.

Anna's school is located off the main highway in a rocky, wooded area hard to get to. Except for an American flag at the top of a huge flagpole outside, one might mistake the school for another hillside barn. The morning I arrived to talk with the children at Anna's invitation, they were gathered around the big pot-bellied stove. Anna had come early and built the fire.

Like so many other Negro rural schools, this one has no library, nor were there any extra books, nor even a newspaper. There was no cafeteria so the children could have a hot lunch. There was no playground equipment. There was a television set provided by one of the new government programs.

The younger Negro teacher had charge of the first four grades in one room, and Anna conducted classes for the upper grades in another. While she conducted classes for one group, the remaining children waited patiently.

Here Anna waits for the inevitable change that will open a new world for her students but in all probability will close hers. She has had no indication that a job will be provided for her. Since this is the only home she knows, it is not likely that she will move. Yet she is so preoccupied with getting the children ready for the great change that she does not have the time, nor does she choose, to consider her own future in the profession to which she has devoted her life.

"Will they know enough?" she asked. "What can I do that I am not doing to help them?" She was concerned about the children's speech. She had them stand and read and spell aloud. She inquired about special programs for the retarded ones. "I want my pupils to be able to do the things I always wanted to do," she said, "and never had an opportunity."

I came away from the school that morning wondering why Anna stayed on, waiting for the last child to leave—and how many more "Anna's" there are in the South. And how many white teachers there are who would show this spirit and dedication and unselfish attitude toward Negro youth.

We, as professional people, are not totally without blame for the condition of the Negro children of the South today. It is no secret that we, too, have more or less ignored Negro education. Instead of leading the way, informing the nation of what had to be done, and should have been done, we have sat back and waited to be told. In a time of great national crisis, the educators have had to follow—letting government and industry tell us what must be done—when we should have led the way. Even our teacher organizations until very recently have been most hesitant to commit themselves.

Of course, now it is becoming popular to help the "disadvantaged" because it is profitable. There is a "grant" for everything nowadays—and so much money that we are having a difficult time spending it. Schools can get more money if they show evidence of supporting "the poor."

And while I know this has been necessary, conditions being what they are—it does not lessen the reflection. I wish it could all have been done without money as the guiding force, but it is not too late. So much is yet to be done. And if we are worthy of our profession, we will waste no time in dedicating ourselves to lifting the cloak of ignorance that has smothered these children for three hundred years.

There are in the South more than 3.5 million Negro children enrolled in the public schools and over five hundred thousand Negro and white teachers. Together we can bring these children out of an abyss of ignorance and deprivation. Each of us will have to do his part in his own community. As Lyndon B. Johnson said in 1962: "No one of us is going to be able to do the job alone, but that is no excuse for dodging our moral obligation to work together. And, working together, we can achieve the goal of equal opportunity for all."

Many of the problems, I know, are beyond the jurisdiction of school personnel. Teachers cannot effect changes in the home, not directly and certainly not immediately. But in the school we can make that child's day so rewarding that in the end it will overcome whatever he returns to at night, and ultimately change it. The knowledge that is acquired through our efforts today will grow from generation to generation and will come back to America threefold. Every Negro child, and every white child, who breaks the barriers of ignorance and poverty today will bring another and still another behind him. In our efforts today to help Negro children realize individual fulfillment lies the hope not only of the Negro race but of our whole society.

This is why everything we do today is of critical importance. The change that comes to one life will bring change to another—and on and on—like a pebble cast into the water, which makes a ripple in the water, and the ripple goes on and on.

So many of the problems of human relations at times do seem insoluble. And yet we have the capacity to dream and hope, and it is in the dreaming and the hoping that the answers will be found. We, as teachers, must do more than hope and dream. We have a professional and a moral obligation to exercise our hopes and dreams. This, I have faith, we shall do. And in so doing, we shall develop a new approach to living—a truly Christian approach—which will bring stature to the South.

Lillian Smith, author of *Strange Fruit* and many other soul-searching books about the South, has said: "The New South? It hasn't quite been born yet. To touch it, you have to reach inside the womb." She knows whereof she speaks. I can tell you, too, that the "New South" is on the way: it is ready to be born. It will only be a "few more days" now, for thousands and thousands of good people are "a-helpin' in the birthin'." The New South is in the hearts and minds of today's children.